THE CRISIS OF
U.S. CAPITALISM
and
THE FIGHT-BACK

International
Publishers
New York

THE CRISIS OF
U.S. CAPITALISM
and
THE FIGHT-BACK

Report to the 21st Convention
of the Communist Party U.S.A.

GUS HALL

LIBRARY OF CONGRESS CATALOGING IN PUBLICATION DATA

Hall, Gus.
  The crisis of U.S. capitalism and the fight-back.

  1. United States—Social conditions—1960-
2. United States—Politics and government—
1969- 3. Communism—United States. I. Title.
HN59.H22   309.1'73   75-25704
ISBN 0-7178-0460-7

ABOUT THE AUTHOR

Gus Hall has been the General Secretary of the Communist Party since 1959 and is an internationally recognized authority on Marxism-Leninism. He is the author of *The Energy Rip-Off, Imperialism Today*, and scores of booklets and articles which have been widely distributed and translated into many languages.

Born in Minnesota, he was one of the founders of the United Steelworkers of America and a leader of the Little Steel Strike in 1937 in Ohio. He was also a member of the International Woodworkers of America, the Laborers International Union of America, and the International Association of Bridge, Structural and Ornamental Ironworkers. He served in the U.S. Navy during World War II.

Joining the Communist Party in 1927, he became an organizer for the Young Communist League, and later the leader of the Communist Party in Ohio, and in 1950 he was the National Secretary of the Communist Party, U.S.A. During the years of the McCarthyite hysteria, in the 1950's he served an 8-year prison term in the Leavenworth Federal Prison under a Smith Act frameup. In 1972 he was the Communist Party's candidate for President, running together with Vice Presidential candidate Jarvis Tyner.

This book contains the text of Gus Hall's main report to the 21st National Convention of the Communist Party held in Chicago on June 26-30, 1975.

CONTENTS

THE CRISIS OF
U.S. CAPITALISM
and
THE FIGHT-BACK

INTRODUCTION
Our Revolutionary Heritage

Dear Delegates, Honored Guests and Comrades:

We welcome the guests who are with us from other lands and we send our regrets to 200 fraternal guests from other lands who wanted to be here but were denied visas. While Kissinger and Ford are busy making demagogic speeches about the "free flow of ideas" and about "the great freedoms of the capitalist state," their State Department sent cables to every country—"no visas." What a sad commentary on this 200th Anniversary of our independence!

We have come back home to Chicago! We convene our 21st National Convention here in the Midwest, which is the pivotal, industrial cluster of our land and the homeplate of our working class. Meeting here in Chicago which is the "germinal spot," the birthplace of our Party, is in a sense an act of rededication to some principles and an act of reaffirmation of some basic truths about our class and our Party.

Yes, from our very inception we have been and we are the revolutionary party of the United States working class.

Yes, from the day of our birth as a party we have been and we are the party of the science of Marxism-Leninism.

Yes, from the day of our organized appearance we have been and we are the party of the victims of racist oppression—the

9

party of Black, Chicano, Puerto Rican, Asian and Native American Indian peoples.

Yes, from the very beginning our Party has been and is the party of class struggle trade unionism, the party of Black and white unity. We have always been and we are the most consistent anti-monopoly force.

Yes, throughout our 56 years, wherever there have been and wherever there are struggles in the interest of the people, Communists have always been and are an active ingredient in these struggles.

From the very first gathering here in Chicago we have been and we are the leading force in the United States for socialism.

Over a half-century ago it was the rising rate of class exploitation and the developing fundamental class contradiction in these basic industries here in the industrial heartland that prepared the soil for the appearance of our Party. The birth of the Communist Party was as inevitable as were the ingots of steel coming down the steel mills. The class struggle was the furnace that molded our Party. The founding members of our Party were all active fighters against injustice everywhere. But more than anything else they were active fighters and leaders of the working class and the trade unions. They had all come through the experiences of being in the IWW, the various militant socialist groups and the anarchists. They were leaders. But they were also the rank and file of the rising trade union movement.

Our Party, the new-born revolutionary infant, was nurtured on the picket lines of striking steelworkers, auto and packinghouse workers, railroad workers, machinists and iron, copper and coal miners.

The forerunners of our Party marched at Haymarket Square. Our comrades led, marched and were wounded and murdered in the Memorial Day Massacre in front of the Chicago and Gary steel plants.

Thus, our new Party was tempered in the jails and prisons. And above all it grew up and matured in the union halls, in the shops and pits.

The Communist Party was conceived and has grown up as the revolutionary working class party. It was conceived as a vanguard party of a class destined by the force of history to lead civilization to the next plateau. It is because we are a party of the working class that our Party represents the best interests of all oppressed, and the best interests of our nation.

It is because we are a working class party that we fight for the unity of all anti-monopoly forces.

It is because we are a party of the working class that we are the most consistent, uncompromising, and effective fighters against racism.

It is because we are a working class party that we are also the most consistent fighters for the equality of women.

It is because we are a working class party that we are a party of the youth.

It is because we are a revolutionary working class party that Communists develop into the best fighters for all reforms that advance the interests of our class and people. We are the best fighters for concessions, for reforms, for putting curbs on monopoly capital. This is because, as to the basic solution, we are for plowing capitalism under and because we are the party of socialism.

It is because we are a working class revolutionary party that we are a party of internationalism.

Here in Chicago, the birthplace of our Party, we renew our commitment, our dedication to our class and to our people. We will redouble our efforts to be deserving of the honored designation, the Communist Party of the USA, the vanguard, revolutionary, Marxist-Leninist party of the working class.

Since our beginnings here in Chicago our Party has come a long way. We can take great pride in our Party's history and in the contributions of our Party. We have overcome many difficulties and obstacles. We can have great confidence in our future.

This is a moment of many anniversaries, including the 200th year of our successful war of liberation. It is also the 125th year since the first Marxist organization was organized in the U.S. It is the 30th anniversary of the defeat of the most brutal, the bloodiest of capitalist dictatorships, Hitler-fascism.

These are historic landmarks in the struggle for social progress. In the struggles and movements of today we build on the best revolutionary heritage of these earlier contributions to human progress.

1. ECONOMIC CRISIS

The people of our rich and productive land face many problems. But clearly the problem that has emerged as the key link in the chain of life is the economic one.

The most critical problem is the devastating effect of the economic crisis. As a result there is a serious deterioration in the quality of life. Square meals are spaced out. Medical and dental care are postponed. Enrollment in a college is cancelled. There is a sense of insecurity, shock, fear and frustration. But the overriding mood is anger and a rising militancy to strike back.

The crisis is adding new notches to the belt of hunger and malnutrition. Living in poverty is a way of life for 37 million people. Millions of the employed have become partly-employed and partly-paid. More of the employed become the unemployed. The lines of those unemployed, who have lived beyond their government designated life span on unemployment insurance have become nonexistent. When they receive their last check their names are simply removed from all of the lists. They are not counted as unemployed and they are not recognized as being part of the labor force either. Following the racist patterns of the last-to-be-hired and first-to-be-fired, the same racist patterns continue among the unemployed who are expunged from all lists and records. They are not even counted in the 10-15% unemployed.

The U.S. is the only major capitalist country in the world that places a cutoff date on how long an unemployed worker can live!

This crisis has branded the youth as a surplus generation. Most of the young people in the ghettos never reach the status of being employed or unemployed. They are condemned to joblessness before they reach the age of employment. Like a hurricane, the crisis is cutting the sharpest path of devastation across the ghettos and barrios of our land. The eye of the economic hurricane is brutally racist.

More of the elderly are dying from malnutrition and lack of medical care than from old age. Under capitalism these are called "natural causes." Not only are the elderly forced to eat dog food, but in New York the rich pay more per day for the upkeep of their dogs in the kennels than the state or city governments spend on the care of the mentally ill or the people on welfare. Over 50% of the elderly live below the poverty level.

The crisis is wiping out the bridgeheads of equality won by working-class women. During each depression, and after each war, capitalism reverts back to holding women as a pool of reserve labor.

This crisis is adding a new dimension to the crisis of the cities. The urban centers are falling apart. Cities have been in crisis conditions for some time. But now many of them are teetering on the brink of bankruptcy. Like New York City, many are living on borrowed time and borrowed finances. The big cities are becoming the decaying slums of the nation, the centers of repression, malnutrition, and corruption.

History does not repeat itself. But big business demagogy does. In the 1930's prosperity was "just around the corner" for many years. Now corporate propagandists want the people to get involved in the game of "is the crisis bottoming out?" We are not going to get into the charades of whether it is bottoming out or not. Such demagogy is for the purpose of directing the attention of the people away from the real problems and away from the struggle.

Our task is to organize mass movements and struggles. The cardinal question for us is not when the crisis will bottom out, but how to develop struggles against the effects of the crisis; how to develop the struggle for jobs on the basis of first priority; how to stop the deterioration of the standard of living; how to make the rich, the banks, and the corporations pay for the crisis they have created, and how to force the government to change priorities.

For the banks and the corporations the crisis has bottomed out at a very high level of profit. For the people there is no bottoming out, only a deterioration in the quality of life. Big business would like to get the people to debate when the crisis is "going to bottom out" while their bottoms are still out.

Our Convention must deal with this most central of all questions, seriously and concretely. We must declare loudly and clearly that not 10%, not 5%, not 3%, not even 1% unemployment is acceptable.

The basis for our approach is simple. An economic system that cannot provide the basic and elementary requirements of a job for all who want to work should itself be bottomed out of existence.

Speaking to a Chamber of Commerce dinner in Detroit a few days ago, the General Motors chairman, who makes a million dollars a years in salary and bonuses alone, said: "No thinking person would abandon the most successful system the world has ever seen until he has a reasonable guarantee that what is promised will be as good."

Well, Mr. Murphy, we are thinking people and we give not only a reasonable guarantee, but an absolute, iron-clad, your-money-back-guarantee that the socialist alternative is not only as good but infinitely better than capitalism.

There is a strange silence from the ranks of the economic

pundits of capitalism. Only yesterday they pompously pontificated on how capitalism, and especially U.S. capitalism, had overcome the problem of economic crises because it was a "neo-capitalism" that was "transformed," "reformed," and is now a "planned," "organized" system without class antagonism, without unemployment or poverty.

There are serious problems flowing from this crisis. And there are also critical new, longer range economic problems that are the products of a deeper deterioration of the foundations of capitalism. There are busy termites in the structural woodwork of capitalism which we will discuss later.

2. THE HISTORIC MOMENT

Each day adds its own evidence that, in point of time, this is the most explosive moment in the history of organized society. It is a moment when the cumulative processes of quantitative evolutionary change have been replaced by a revolutionary qualitative transformation. In a sense the world is being reborn. Human society is in the process of being basically restructured. The old system in decay, with all of its anti-human values, is now being rejected by a majority of the world's people. Open defenders of capitalism are fast becoming an extinct species.

Socialism is the new power base of human progress, the new political, economic and ideological magnet. It daily demonstrates the superiority of a system, structured and motivated for the sole purpose of serving all of the people, a society that legislates against and frowns on private profit as a goal in life. This magnificent transformation is both quantitative and qualitative. It is evolutionary and revolutionary. On the scales of history, the direction and the process are irreversible. For anyone tuned in, it is very clear that the rhythm of the struggle for social progress is progressive and upbeat. And for us, of the greatest significance is the fact that we are at a point in time when all of the forces and factors propelling this transition are reaching new levels and new stages of development. We are also at a point in time when all of these processes have shifted to higher gears. There is a new tempo, a new explosiveness to all social, economic, and political processes. That which was a trend yesterday is today's reality.

To keep up with the times is to recognize the new stage and the new tempo of this historic transition. Not to recognize or not to understand this element of today's reality is to be out of step—is to tail events.

The main contradiction of this epoch—the epoch of the most fundamental turning point in history—is between socialism and capitalism. The lines for this confrontation were drawn, and the gauntlet was thrown down, with the birth of the first socialist state, the Soviet Union. During the epoch, the confrontation between these two systems has been the main factor in shaping world history. From the moment the Putilov factory workers scaled the walls of the decaying Czarist empire, for world imperialism, the guilding principle for its policies and actions, has been the political, ideological and physical destruction of socialism. This has always superceded all other desires of imperialism.

At every turn of events, imperialism has returned to the preparations and implementation of this principal class objective. This has significance because today there is a new reality. Today the main cardinal factor determining the direction of human events is the qualitative shift in the balance between these two opposite forces of this epoch—the challenger has become the champion and the comeback trail for aging imperialism is largely closed.

As the balance has shifted, it has increasingly become more difficult for imperialism to implement its policies, based on the destruction of socialism. That, which from its class viewpoint remains desirable, has become increasingly impractical and impossible.

The tides of history are now with socialism. The essence of imperialist initiatives is aggression. As imperialism has lost its dominating influence, the options for its initiatives continue to narrow down. It is in a position where it is forced to react to events. In most parts of the world imperialism is frustrated and on the defensive. And in most parts of the world it is the forces of progress that are on the offensive.

This correct understanding of the nature of the relationship of forces should of course not lead anyone to complacency. Imperialism retreats, it maneuvers, but it does not give up.

There are some imperialist "crazies" who would rather see the world destroyed than to see the final defeat of capitalism.

In its post-Vietnam editorial, the *Wall Street Journal* said it again: "The main threat remains the thrust of the Soviet Union." The designs and desires of imperialism remain. Therefore, it continues as a source of danger.

Wherever imperialism finds a weakness, it penetrates. Therefore, vigilance is necessary. When imperialism is blocked in one form, it seeks out new forms. Therefore, anti-imperialism must be ready to shift to the new fields of battle.

But all of these activities take place in the context that imperialism cannot now force its will. It cannot now force its policies on the world. That fact is the cardinal question, when we consider the point of time, the time of day in the epoch of history's greatest turning point.

3. THE GENERAL CRISIS

A fundamental process of this epoch is the deterioration, the degeneration, of world capitalism. This general decaying crisis of capitalism is generated by its internal contradictions based on its inner laws of development. But it is also directly influenced by external forces—in the first place by the rising power of world socialism, by a working class moving to fulfill its designated role, by victorious movements and struggles of national liberation.

The process of decay has gone through several qualitative changes called stages. Some may again ask: Why again go into these seemingly abstract assessments? The answer is that they are not abstract questions. The fact that this decay of capitalism has reached a new stage is of the greatest significance. It is the very core of the reality to which we have to respond.

Our strategic concepts, our tactics must reflect a specific class enemy with specific weaknesses and strengths. Also, this has become a crucial matter because now the general crisis has reached a point where it affects all aspects of life in the U.S., and to one degree or another it is a critical factor in all of the capitalist countries. It affects and influences current economic patterns, politics, ideology, and culture. Consequently, it has a weighty presence in the everyday affairs of the class struggle.

The general crisis deepens because there simply are no possible basic or longer range solutions to the problems of society under capitalism. This is now true even in the richest and strongest of the capitalist countries. Capitalism is simply not for these times. It is as simple as that. This is true because the basic contradiction of the capitalist mode of production sharpens the class contradiction which then gives rise to a more united, a more advanced working class movement.

The general crisis deepens because capitalism has failed, and fails, to reach its most basic of all goals, its efforts to stop or to destroy world socialism. It is a frustrated beast. The opportunity, if it ever existed, for such a turn of events, has long since receded into history.

The general crisis deepens because the last of the old colonial empires is crumbling.

The general crisis deepens because capitalism fails to move the liberated countries towards the capitalist path of development. It has no new areas of expansion.

The crisis deepens with the development of state monopoly capitalism. The general crisis deepens because while the measures and regulations of state monopoly capitalism may be of momentary benefit to some sectors, they not only do not solve the fundamental problems but even add to the chaos, the anarchy, the contradiction, and antagonism within capitalism.

The crisis deepens because for world capitalism the growth rate is bottoming out. Its reserves are being depleted. Militarization, the tendency of continuous inflation, are features of the deepening crisis. There is a collapse of the capitalist world financial structure. Gold and the currencies of the capitalist countries are being replaced by toilet tissue money. The continuing economic and political instability are all products of the general crisis, but they in turn add their bit to the further deepening of the crisis. What is new is that there is a new quality, a new qualitative stage, to all these processes, resulting in a new overall stage of the crisis.

Victories over imperialism

The victories over imperialism are charted on a rising curve. Each day adds new strength to the working class movements of the world. Anti-imperialism has become the broadest mass trend. This epoch will close the books on colonialism. Each victory has its own direct effect on its immediate surroundings. But the totality of events adds up to a new qualitative force that is determining the course of human events.

The successes in the building of socialism in each of the countries has its own significance. But the continuing achievements of the socialist countries in building socialism, and the continuing decay of the capitalist world, adds a new quality to the competition between the two world systems. Because of this, the comparison of the overall quality of life between the two systems has itself become an important factor influencing the historic transition from capitalism to socialism. This continues to add its force to the general crisis of capitalism.

United States imperialism

For U.S. imperialism this moment in time continues to be a period of setbacks, retreats and maneuvers that generally end in new frustrations. The basic cause for the frustrations of U.S. imperialism is that the options for aggression are being blocked. Some of the difficulties of U.S. imperialism are related to what Lenin correctly said was the law of uneven development of capitalism. But to be a negative recipient of that law when imperialism is in a deep crisis, and has lost its position of determining human events, is quite different from the effects of that law in earlier periods. More accurately, the present situation and its effects on U.S. imperialism are guided by the law of uneven deterioration of capitalism.

Because of the setbacks the debate grows as to whether the United States remains a first rate power. Whether it is or not is not of too much practical significance. But as long as some of the monopoly propagandists debate the question we would like to suggest a proper framework for the debate. The question should be limited to whether the United States is a first rate capitalist power. Then the answer is obvious. The United States is a first rate power, but within a second rate socio-economic system. Each should be judged within their own league.

The direction, the main essence of the trends of this epoch are clearly sketched by the explosive current events, the rising curve in the building of socialism. The fact that the Soviet Union alone now produces over 20% of all the world's industrial production is of tremendous significance. The main current and direction of history is emerging in the new realities of Vietnam, Cambodia, Laos, Portugal, Guinea Bissau, Angola, Greece, and at the United Nations. These trends are dramatically underlined by the great exciting victory of the Communist Party of Italy, winning 33.5 per cent of the popular vote for the Communist candidates. That is a historic development. Symbolic of these new trends, Mozambique at this very hour has won its independence.

After 50 years of continuous struggle against the imperialist forces of France, Japan and then for the last 21 years against the brutal aggression of U.S. imperialism, Vietnam is now at peace, free, independent and on the road to unity.

The U.S. military intervention into Cambodia has boomeranged. All of the maneuvering, the years of the most brutal, secret bombing, and the massive infiltration of the CIA has not stopped the people of Laos from winning their right to self-determination.

Eisenhower expressed the worst fears of imperialism, and they have become a reality. The U.S. corporations, the Rockefellers and their Exxons have lost the rich oil resources. They have been forced to close their banks. Chase Manhattan Bank now has no friends in Indo-China. And as Ike said, "They have lost all those rich resources down there."

These victories in Indochina are of special significance because they slam the door on imperialism and not only in separate countries, but on a whole new section of the globe. South East Asia is now off limits for imperialism for all times. These victories have a special meaning for the people of the U.S., first because they are direct defeats for U.S. imperialism and, second, because millions of our people in unprecedented numbers were actively involved in the 12-year struggle against this aggression.

We can be very proud of this contribution. Our Party can be very proud of its unique and special contribution of leadership in this struggle. We gave the struggle an anti-imperialist direction. We brought into it a working-class outlook. We were the most consistent force for unity. We, more than any other force, warned and steered it away from sectarian blind alleys, from the provocateurs and enemy agents.

Ford, Kissinger and Westmoreland have given public testimony about the effectiveness of this struggle. And it is true, whenever you can make warhawks say, "We are frustrated," you are being effective. They are frustrated because finally 83% of the people were against all further military involvement. They were frustrated because mass sentiment had resulted in a law limiting the president's war-making powers in Vietnam, Laos and Cambodia. These are expressions of a deep anti-imperialist sentiment.

Anti-imperialism has become a significant mass phenomenon in the U.S. Under the specific circumstances these factors frustrated the Ford Administration. Without them undoubtedly the bombing of Vietnam would have been resumed. In fact when the Ford Administration was trying to change the law, the bombing fleets were being readied for action.

But to this one must add that the criminal acts of provocation and the brutal military acts that followed against Cambodia around the Mayaguez must serve as a warning. There can be acts of desperation and acts of provocation by the Doctor Strangeloves—the Kissingers, Westmorelands, and Schlesingers.

But the Mayaguez affair boomeranged against imperialism. The world sees it as an action of a defeated and frustrated bully.

For years the fascist rulers of Portugal, with the support of U.S. imperialism, resisted the world trends. They fought to keep their colonial empire in Africa and the fascist rule in Portugal. But the end came dramatically and simultaneously to both. The self-interests of the people of Africa and the people of Portugal merged and gave birth to movements and a struggle against the fascist colonial rulers. Neither Africa nor Europe will ever be the same.

These developments have forced the questions of putting an end to colonial, racist oppression in all of Africa on the order of the day. They have forced the racist regimes of South Africa and Rhodesia to maneuver and retreat.

The events in Indochina, the collapse of the colonial empire of Portugal in Africa and the smashing of the fascist rule in Portugal, bring to light some new relationships reflecting the new phenomena in the world. These struggles show a new relationship between national liberation and socialism. There is a new relationship between the countries of socialism and the forces of national liberation. But there is also a new relationship, and in many cases an overlapping, between the struggle for national liberation and the struggle for socialism within each country. There is a closer association of the anti-imperialist, anti-fascist, and anti-capitalist trends. There is a new cohesiveness between all of the movements fighting for human progress.

This trend towards closer kinship is a reflection of changes in the role of classes and ideologies. They come about because of the increasing leadership role of the working class in the world and in all of these movements. In these developments, it is clear, the working class has moved to fulfill its historic leading role. This is an important new element in all of the struggles today.

This trend of unity is a reflection of the new level of the influence of socialism. The example of the building of socialism is a new force in all struggles. And finally the trend takes place because of the increasing influences of the science of Marxism-Leninism and the Communist Parties in all movements. On the other side of the coin, these new trends of unity are evidence of the decline of the influence of bourgeois ideology, a decline of the influence of petty bourgeois concepts, including the bankruptcy and the decline in the influence of Maoism. All this adds a new quality to the struggles of the epoch. There is a closer kinship between these developments and movements because they are all related to the present new phase of the historic transition from capitalism to socialism. The new unity provides new strength to the forces propelling the world revolutionary process.

At moments when the winds and currents are more favorable it is always wise to be aware and to warn against possible gales and countercurrents. The jingoistic orgy that accompanied the seizure of the Mayaguez should serve as a warning. Only an alert and organized movement; only a worldwide anti-imperialist unity can continue to keep the forces of U.S. imperialism frustrated.

It is true U.S. imperialism is frustrated and it is forced to retreat, but it remains the arsenal for the forces of world reaction, the arsenal for the military fascist dictatorships and the reactionary colonial rulers the world over. It exports more arms than the rest of the world together. It is still the ideological citadel of world reaction. And now it is clear also that it is the lair of the assassins, the home base of the hit-men of imperialism.

The latest expose reveals U.S. imperialism also as the main source, the cesspool of corruption that is defiling the lifeline of the capitalist world. It has a system of illegal, under-the-table payoffs for which there is no precedent. To those of us who have no illusions about capitalism this is no surprise. The corporate-political slush funds at home and the system of political corruption, payoffs and assassinations overseas are but a phase of the new level of the decay of capitalism. They operate like the gangsters they are, who have lost all possibility of winning public support for their operations or ideas. Assassins move in when ideology and politics have failed. There has always been an overlapping and an exchange of personnel between the corporations and the government and the military. Now there is a fourth source of cadre for the personnel exchange—the gangsters, the hipsters of the underworld. And why not? They are all in the same business. They mix because they are of the same species.

The CIA is and has been in the business of political assassination overseas. It is directly responsible for and involved in the political assassination of tens of thousands of political leaders in Vietnam and other countries.

Now it is also clear that the FBI is and has been in the business of political assassinations at home. This is obvious even from the minimum admissions of the Department of Justice that the FBI actively worked as provocateurs to get Communists assassinated by gangster elements. This is all in keeping with a class that is being defeated and therefore takes measures of desperation. We are now going to court demanding all of the material related to persecution, including the murder plots against our Party.

The events in Chile continue as proof that imperialism never gives up. The U.S. policy of aggression by the CIA and State Department and the direct action of U.S.-based multi-national corporations in Chile are daily warnings to all of the countries in Latin America. The U.S. policy toward Chile is not an isolated case. U.S. imperialism is pursuing the same policies toward all of the countries in Latin America.

We are seeing some seemingly contradictory lines of development in the U.S. policy toward Latin America. The State Department, CIA and Pentagon continue to support the most reactionary, fascist military forces in every country. On the other hand, they are moving to lift the trade embargo imposed against Cuba. This contradiction in policy is only tactical. Kissinger's tactics

are a testimony to the support for and the popularity of the
Cuban revolution amongst the countries and peoples of Central and South America. It has become difficult to do any kind
of business in any of these countries if one has an open position
of aggression against people's Cuba. We must see the lifting of
the trade embargo as a first step in the struggle to put an end
to all the policies of aggression against Cuba.

There is also some progress as well as some new signs of
danger in the Mideast. U.S. imperialism continues its efforts
to keep Israel as a base of operations against the Arab peoples
and countries. But it is also building bases of operations in the
oil producing countries. This is the essence of Kissinger's shuttle
diplomacy. It is a shuttle for U.S. oil profits.

U.S. imperialism ships billions of dollars worth of arms to
Israel. But there is now also growing a number of military,
intelligence, and ideological establishments in countries like Iran
and Saudi Arabia in which the Pentagon and the CIA have
major and even decisive influence. These U.S.-sponsored and
largely operated bases are a danger to all of the people of the
Mideast, but they are a special danger to the forces of anti-
imperialism in all of the countries. These are new bases of
operation for U S. imperialism. They raise new dangers to the
struggle for national liberation and independence being waged
by the countries in the Middle East. U.S. imperialism works
both sides of the street. But the goal is profits from oil.

We are in a sense at a critical point because the problems in
the Middle East are now ripe for a peaceful solution. But
Kissinger and Ford cannot be trusted as the midwives of peace
in the Mideast. They are for peace only if the profits of oil keep
flowing to the Rockefellers. A just and lasting peace can only
be worked out at a reconvened conference in Geneva.

The CIA and the U.S. multi-national corporations it serves
are busy in many countries of the world. But right now they
are the busiest in Africa. They are the assassins, provocateurs,

and the corrupters on the African scene. They are vigorously pursuing the policies of divide and rule.

The main support base for the racist regimes of South Africa and Rhodesia is U.S. imperialism. Without such support these regimes would collapse. It is because of this that the work of the National Anti-Imperialist Movement in Solidarity with African Liberation, including the petition to expel South Africa from the United Nations, is of decisive importance. It hits at the main lifeline of reaction and racism in Africa.

In this new period, as U.S. imperialism has been forced to retreat from areas of open aggression, it increases its efforts by other means. It is putting greater emphasis on covert activities. The buying off and corrupting of politicians within foreign governments has reached a new level. The exposure of some of the activities of the United Brands, Exxon, Lockheed, Gulf, and Northrop, etc., gives some idea of the efforts of corruption and payoff.

One of the lessons of Chile is that the anti-imperialist forces, especially in the U.S., must place a higher priority on exposing these new forms of imperialist penetration and activities.

From all of this, in spite of setbacks, U.S. imperialism continues in its efforts to ride two horses going in the opposite directions. Some significant steps of detente have already been won, but the Ford-Kissinger-Rockefeller-Schlesinger Administration would still like to have it both ways—detente and aggression.

They are taking part in the SALT talks, while the Pentagon is hell-bent on readying the nuclear arsenal for a first-strike capacity. In fact it is this criminal U.S. policy of building for a strike-first nuclear capacity that is the only real obstacle to an agreement on reducing the level of offensive nuclear weapons. They take part in negotiations to cut arms, but demand the largest war budget in history. They say they support the concept of a European Security peace treaty, but they prod the capitalist countries of Europe to upgrade NATO's military establishment. Ford and Kissinger talk about friendship with the Soviet Union, but the U.S. ideological organs, led by the *New York Times,* are conducting the most vicious anti-Soviet campaign—in some ways worse than in the days of the cold war. They talk about increasing trade with the socialist countries, but they are doing nothing to lift the restrictions on that trade.

The Ford-Kissinger-Rockefeller-Schlesinger theme song is that the United States can negotiate, can have detente only if it continues building an ever stronger military force. The logic of this is that the United States is going to try to deal from a position of strength. This was the disastrous logic of the cold war. It is a policy built on a miscalculation. It will not lead to detente.

It is a miscalculation because there is no way in hell that U.S. imperialism is going to have its way. No amount of overkill on top of overkill is going to change this reality. Detente and $105 billion war budgets move in opposite directions. It is in this context of contradiction that we must consider and take up the struggle for detente.

Detente

The pressure of the pro-war forces to return to the outlook of the cold war, the waverings of all sectors of monopoly capital and the wishy-washiness of the liberals only make it more urgent to increase efforts in the struggle for detente. The struggle for detente is an ongoing and continuous battle. The struggle for detente is the right concept at the right moment and in the right epoch. To expect imperialism to accept detente willingly and without a struggle is to live in a world of illusions.

Thus, it is in the dialectics of the struggle within the context of the new balance that now exists between the two socio-economic systems that the struggle for detente must be assessed and understood.

The struggle for detente is both correct and urgently necessary. To be able to put up the most effective fight for detente it is necessary to understand what it is and what it is not. In a very basic sense detente is a struggle against imperialist aggression at a moment when it has lost its ability to dominate human events. It is a struggle to give the concept of peaceful coexistence the force of agreement and international law. The struggle for detente is to force imperialism to conform to the new balance of world forces.

Thus, in September there will be a world conference in Havana in solidarity with Puerto Rico in its struggle for independence from U.S. imperialism. This was initiated by the World Peace Council and stimulated by the United Nations resolution declaring that Puerto Rico is in a colonial status. This strengthened the struggle for independence. This was advanced by the socialist states with Cuba playing an important role. Needless to say, the world conference in Havana is of special significance for us in the United States. We must take concrete measures to set up local united committees and work for mass delegations to participate in this conference. It is related to and is part of the struggle for detente. It puts the struggle for Puerto Rican independence into the world scene.

Detente is the struggle to prevent a nuclear disaster, to keep the world away from the brink, from being turned into a pile of ashes. It is a struggle to put a cap on—to cut or even to slow down—the bottomless, endless arms race. It is a struggle to scrap the U.S. imperialist restrictions on trade with the socialist countries. It is a struggle to create an atmosphere of sanity and to cut down on world tensions.

Again, the World Peace Council, at a meeting in Stockholm, initiated a call for "a new world-wide offensive against the arms race." They call for banning all nuclear and other weapons of mass destruction, for general and complete disarmament, for a United Nations World Disarmament Conference to "stop the arms race." This move will be welcomed by millions of people in this country. Such a world program can help us in our struggle to cut the military budget and to make funds available for social needs. With its origin in Stockholm, this campaign can be put on the scale of the Stockholm Peace Petition twenty-five years ago. This also reflects and strengthens the struggle to make detente irreversible. We should welcome such a mass campaign for peace.

Now, it is difficult to imagine who in his right mind cannot see the importance of detente. And there are also some other positives that flow from detente. The struggle for detente cramps the style and cuts the effectiveness of anti-Communist, anti-Soviet, and generally anti-socialist propaganda. A. Sobolev of the Institute of Marxism-Leninism in the USSR placed this well:

> It becomes increasingly difficult in the course of peaceful coexistence for capitalism to use various extraordinary measures to solve their contradictions. That is why peaceful coexistence does not lead to the weakening of the contradictions of capitalism, but in the long run, if one can put it this way, locks capitalism's social economic relations within the framework of its natural laws, on which soil its contradictions develop most fully.

The socialist countries are working-class powers. They are setting an example of life without racism, without crises, without unemployment. Detente with such working-class powers influences the struggle in the capitalist countries. It is not accidental that most of the people who are fighting against detente are also the most reactionary, racist and anti-democratic in domestic affairs. The struggle for detente is the most effective struggle for the self-interests of the working class and of national liberation within the world arena. It is a struggle to create the best, the most advantageous conditions for the class struggle and the overall movement for social progress.

It is a correct and a winning policy for a class that has emerged on the world stage not only as the leading class, but as the decisive force determining the direction of human events.

Detente has the support of the majority of the people of the world. But there are forces who oppose it. And there are some who are confused. Therefore, for those who are confused let us put on the table what detente is not. Detente is not a love-pact between capitalism and socialism. It is not a scheme to reconcile the two systems. It is not a blueprint for the convergence of the two systems. It is not an attempt to paper over the evils of the capitalist system in the capitalist countries.

In the first place, this is an impossibility because the roots of the class struggle are in the system of exploitation, within each country. Detente is not an agreement to accept or to turn one's head away from the oppression by imperialism anywhere. Comrade Leonid Brezhnev made this clear in a public statement here when he stated: "The Soviet Union's support for all national liberation struggles and movements is non-negotiable."

In other words, it is not even up for discussion. After the victories in Indochina, Kissinger in one of his brooding moments dramatically declared: "The U.S. will never forget who gave the arms to Vietnam." We can only hope that he has finally learned one of the new facts of this epoch—that there is a close relationship between the socialist countries and the struggles for national liberation. The movements for national liberation are going to get food, machinery, clothing, medicine, political and diplomatic support—and they are going to get arms.

It is interesting, but not one bit surprising, that both the imperialist ultra-right and the Maoist phony-left now say detente is a scheme by the Soviet Union to export revolution to establish its "hegemony." Of course the Maoists try to have it both ways. When they think they have a left audience they say detente is "the new opportunism prettifying imperialism." When they have the ear of the imperialist spokesmen they warn them about the Soviets attempting to "export revolution." This has now become their main line. The other left line is only for cover-up—something for their phony-left followers to quote to left audiences.

The imperialist ultra-right and the Maoist phony-left are not confused. They are against detente. They are for a return to the cold war. But if one is confused about exporting revolution one can also be confused about detente. As Marxists, we do not base our policies or our hopes on the importing or exporting of revolutions, and we do not do so for very practical reasons.

It is impossible to export revolutions, with or without detente. Revolutionary ideas and the example of the results of revolutions can and do cross state and national boundaries. Support for revolutionary movements is a part of Communist and working-class internationalism. This goes on with or without detente. From this viewpoint the charge of the ultra-right and phony-left is a calculated falsehood intended to mislead the uninformed.

On the other hand, while detente does not export revolutions, it is a very definite obstacle to the exporting of counter-revolutions. In this department the struggle for detente has an impressive list of achievements. There is an inner-logic to all positions. People on the left who join the ultra-right in the struggle against detente will invariably become passive camp-followers of imperialism because the struggle for detente is a struggle against imperialism, and any struggle against detente is a plus for imperialism. In the context of today's world it is difficult, if not impossible, to be for world peace and against detente, because detente is the struggle for peace in the realities of today. The struggle for detente is the only basis for the broadest unity of the forces of peace. The struggle for detente at this moment in time is the centerpiece in the struggle against world imperialism, for world peace and social progress.

It is a contradiction in terms to be against imperialism and for national liberation and also to be against detente. The struggle for detente is a struggle that declares to imperialism: "You are not now the dominating force. The world is not going to accept your dictates. We are insisting on new rules

for the game, new rules that take into account the change
in the balance of world forces."

In all struggles there are weaknesses. But weaknesses can
be corrected. One should not be against struggles because
there are weaknesses. Some say the struggle for detente creates
illusions about imperialism changing its spots. The logic of that
argument would be to never fight for reforms because even
to demand concessions opens the door to the illusion that it
may be possible to change the system by winning concessions.
Reformism breeds such illusions. But not to fight for reforms
because of the danger that it creates illusions leads to phrase-
mongering. In a sense it is political idiocy. It is Trotskyism.
Not to fight and struggle for reforms in the factories, mines
and mills on the basis that they create illusions about the boss
would be a deadend street of condemning exploitation but
doing nothing about it. The same logic applies in the struggle
against imperialism. Not to fight for partial demands because
of the problem of illusions inevitably leads to dehydration of
politics.

Some say that because of detente the socialist countries do not always criticize sharply enough the actions and
statements of imperialism. At specific moments this may be so.
But that does not change the fact that in the international
arena, in the struggle for detente, the socialist countries are
making a historic contribution to the class struggle, to the
struggle against imperialism, and of course, in the struggle for
world socialism.

Each for their own specific purposes, the imperialist ultra-
right, the Maoist phony-left, and the leadership of the Zionist
movements are the anti-detente confluence, the hard core of
the pro-cold war, pro-imperialist forces of today. Each for their
own reasons operate in the cold war orbit mouthing cold war
demagogy, searching for provocations.

The Maoist leadership parades around with the mantle of
representing the interests of the "third world" and that it

"speaks for the movements of Asia, Africa and Latin America."
That in itself is an expression of great power chauvinism. And
the truth is that the movements and political forces of these
continents have rejected and repudiated the Maoist concepts,
including at the Conference of Non-Aligned Nations, held in
Algeria a year ago. And only a week ago there was a conference of all of the Communist Parties of Latin America in
Havana, Cuba which in its main political document, *Latin
America in the Struggle Against Imperialism, for National Independence, Democracy, People's Welfare, Peace and Socialism,* condemned the actions of the Maoists in the following no
uncertain terms:

> This Conference energetically condemns the foreign policy
> of the leadership of the Communist Party of China which
> flirts with Yankee imperialism, defends its presence in Asia
> and in Europe, justifies NATO, stimulates West-German im-
> perialism and revanchism, attacks and slanders the USSR
> with the same viciousness of the worst spokesmen of inter-
> national reaction, fosters the aggressive militarism of the
> world bourgeoisie against it, promotes the insane policy of
> cold war against the heroic Soviet people and, in Latin
> America, has its most ominous expression in the shameless
> connivance with the Chilean Military Junta to which it gives
> political support over the blood of thousands of communists,
> socialists, and other patriots murdered by the brutal repres-
> sion of the fascist tyranny. The Chinese leadership also
> fosters everywhere groups of pseudo-revolutionaries who,
> from a false radicalism, divide the left, attack the Com-
> munist Parties, obstruct progressive processes and frequently
> act as enemy agents within the revolutionary movement.
>
> To confront this policy of treason against unity, solidarity
> and the best traditions of the world revolutionary movement
> is a duty for all the Communist Parties of Latin America.

The struggle for detente on our part is a struggle for a U.S.
foreign policy that is in every way in the best possible in-

terest of the people of the United States. The essence of this struggle is to:

—Close all U.S. foreign bases the world over;

—Block all attempts to return to the cold war;

—Frustrate all attempts of military aggression;

—Block all aid to the racist-military and fascist dictatorships;

—Put an end to all economic and trade blockades;

—Cancel the huge war appropriation;

—Sign the SALT agreements;

—Open up trade with all countries on the basis ef equality; and

—We now want to renew our demand of three years ago— padlock the CIA, FBI and the Pentagon buildings. I believe millions are beginning to agree with us.

In concrete terms for us, this is the essence of the struggle for detente. We must continue, we must improve our contributions to this historic struggle.

4. THE DOMESTIC TRENDS

The Draft Main Political Resolution correctly states that the developments on the domestic scene are related to and are deeply affected by the new stage of the general crisis of capitalism, by the setbacks suffered by U.S. imperialism in the world arena, and by the overall shift in the balance of world forces.

In taking a measure of the period ahead for the U.S., it is necessary to keep in mind that these general factors affecting the course of events are not momentary or cyclical. They are, as the World War II saying goes, "here for the duration."

The present economic crisis has greatly aggravated all problems. When it abates it is going to leave behind it serious economic problems, including a higher level of unemployment. The standard of living will continue to decline; inflation is already taking on a new head of steam, and taxes and rents will continue upward. The present economic crisis is not over, but there are already factors building up that will lead to new cyclical crises. In a sense, at this stage of capitalist developments the booms of the economic cycles will be "boomlets" and the busts will be more continuous. For capitalism, there are no periods of economic stabilization left. That is one of the new features of the new stage of the general crisis. There are indications that U.S. capitalism will follow the downhill developments of the past decade of British and French capitalism.

What are some of the factors that add up to a longer-range forecast of a deterioration of U.S. capitalism? For one, U.S. capitalism is running out of some of its traditional reserves. This includes many of the easily available and cheap raw materials. This includes the negative effects of the U.S.-based, multinational corporate operations. And, as we have stated before, the shift in the balance of world forces against imperialism has a very special effect on U.S. capitalism.

But of course the main aggravating factors are the policies of monopoly capital. The main enemy, the real threat to the well being of the people and the nation, comes from this source. And as monopoly tightens its grip on all phases of life it becomes an ever greater threat to the people, economically and politically.

The bank takeover of the industrial complex, the development of the conglomerates and the multi-nationals, has placed the controlling operations of the economy even further out of sight and out of reach. Because of this they are even more unresponsive to the people's or the nation's needs. This is giving rise to a new kind of alienation and a new level of parasitism. Without adding any values the banks and other institutions of finance now annually collect, on a top priority basis, about $35 to $40 billion dollars as interest on the bonds and loans the government agencies owe them.

The financial-military-industrial complex has become the pivotal center of the state monopoly capitalist structure, feeding itself on the $100 billion-plus war budgets. As was expected by way of Watergate, this state monopoly structure has reached a new level of inner-corruption resulting in a new level of monopoly dictatorial political control of the state and the two old parties. The guiding principle for the operations of monopoly capital today is that the standard of living of the people of the U.S. is too high, wage raises are out of control, and that the expectations of the people have reached beyond realistic limits. This is the guiding principle of the Ford Administration, the Republican Party and most of the Democrats.

In the field of economics, the Ford Administration is now continuing where the Nixon Administration left off. Like Nixon, Ford is now vetoing all measures and impounding funds that in any way would alleviate the problems of the people. On a single day in June, Ford, Rockefeller and Schlesinger all congratulated Congress for upholding Ford's veto of a bill that would have created jobs. They hailed this as "a great historic victory." And, on the very same day, they declared that they will fight anyone who dares to cut one penny from the $100 billion war budget. The veto was based on the demagogy of cutting back on government spending. This day in June must be designated as a day of infamy. More than anything else, it characterizes the basic outlook of the Ford Administration and of monopoly capital—that the defeat of a law that would have created jobs is a "great historic victory."

Ford's "great victory" was against the poor, the unemployed. It was a victory for racism. It is difficult to find the words that adequately describe such anti-human, criminal behavior.

This is the meaning of Ford's constant reference to "the agenda for the future." The agenda is to cut the social welfare and security programs, to cut off stamps, veterans benefits, Medicare, old age benefits. But the agenda also calls for the elimination of all restrictions on corporate profits. It calls for the elimination of all safeguards on the job and of the environment. It is an agenda of corporate profits before people—before health, clean air or the future welfare in general.

The Ford-corporate agenda envisages more production by a smaller work force by way of speedup resulting in a higher rate of unemployment. It calls for cuts in wage rates through part-time employment and the cancellation of wage increases.

On the agenda of monopoly capital is a continuation of the inflation ripoff. The Ford Administration and the oil corporations have just announced a new round of gasoline shortages and price increases. As we predicted in *The Energy Ripoff*, the oil corporations are using their total grip on the refining facilities to create shortages for the purpose of jacking up the prices. So there is a glut of raw fuel but a shortage of gasoline and fuel oil.

The Ford agenda calls for the financial strangulation of the cities as a way of cutting back on education, health, housing and social services. And it calls for cutting back on the "high expectations of the people." An economic system that views people's expectations for a better life as a threat has outlived its usefulness.

The urban centers are being strangled by the banks and the federal government. Local governments in 75 metropolitan areas (where more than 50% of the people of the U.S. live) receive less than 15% of all the money going to government bodies. The hog-share of this money of course goes to the federal government and its $100 billion war budget.

New York City has just been forced into receivership through the so-called "Big Mac" arrangement. The banks are now going to directly determine what every city department gets. They are now not only getting double interest, (first on their past loans and now a whopping 8% interest on bonds to pay the interest to themselves on the old city bonds), but they will also have direct control of taxes that come into the city. For the banks, it is like the traditional double-layer "Big Mac" hamburger—a double-digit "Big Mac." It is a profit windfall for the banks. This is in the tradition of the loan-shark gangsters with their compounded double interest rates. The New York City Administration and the City Council, because in their own petty politics they are footstools of big business, collapsed and now behave like the lackeys they are. New York City is in bankruptcy like Detroit. Cleveland, San Francisco and Atlanta are not far behind.

The struggle for the cities must be placed in the framework of a struggle against the monopolies and the huge war budgets.

As a crisis measure, why not cancel, or declare a moratorium, on all payments of bonds, loans and the interest on them? And why not a capital levy to recover the billions stolen from the public?

The Ford-monopoly agenda to cut back on the standard of living and the quality of life generally, also calls for repression of all dissent or resistance to their attacks on the people. The leading cutting edge of this anti-democratic drive is racism. The strangulation of New York City, Detroit, Gary and the other big urban centers in which there are large ghettos and barrios is, in itself, an act of racism. The continual impounding and vetoing of funds for construction, for housing, education, jobs, and other social needs are features of the racist agenda.

A case study of the racism of this agenda is North Carolina. Of the 70 people on death row, 50 are Black. The most violent and intensive racist campaign is being waged in this state. The Wilmington Ten, including Reverend Ben Chavis, are now closer to being forced to serve a total of 282 years in prison.

The general results of this racist repression in North Carolina are also a case study of racism. The wages of the production workers are the lowest in the country, and only 8% of these workers are members of unions. Racism and the anti-labor, right-to-work laws are pushed by the same monopoly forces. This should serve as a deep lesson for the working class as a whole—that racism is a special feature added to the system of class exploitation resulting in super-profits.

The racist attacks in Boston are a part of the agenda. From their very beginning Ford rushed to give his presidential blessings to the hoodlums in Boston.

Using the economic crisis as a cover, the campaign of deportation of so-called "workers without documents" has taken on new dimensions. If not halted, at the present rate over one and a half million people of Latin American origin will be deported in this vicious campaign. Most of those being deported are of Mexican descent. Massive raids into factories have become a commonplace occurrence in this drive. The struggle to end these roundups and the shipping of people across the borders must become a part of the overall struggle against racism and repression.

On the agenda of repression is a serious danger that Congress will pass a law that will replace the notorious Smith Act. It is a law (designated S-1) that is anti-Communist, anti-labor and racist. The concept behind this legislation is a feature of the Nixon conspiracy to subvert and scrap the Constitution. It is a codification of Nixon's Huston Plan. This plan in turn was inspired by the fascist regulations in Germany and Italy. It would give a blank check to the FBI, CIA, IRS, the immigration border guards, and all public officials to commit crimes and cover up crimes; to wiretap, raid, seize-and-search; to entrap with bombings and murders and put the blame on others; to shoot first, to commit more racist violence—all of this with immunity. It would legalize all the crimes of Watergate. It would revive McCarthyism. All this would be done on the basis that it is just reforming and bringing up to date the criminal code. That Senate Bill S-1 must be defeated. That is a number one task.

As the contradictions of monopoly capital sharpen, the inherent tendencies toward reactionary positions become more pronounced. We must work to keep the lessons of Watergate alive. Watergate was a high-water mark of a process and a conspiracy that was leading to the destruction of democracy. The central lesson of Watergate is that there are powerful forces of monopoly capital who see the traditional democratic structure and the democratic political institutions as obstacles to their class operations in the present stage of developments. And what is most important is that these forces have not given up.

They have been temporarily dispersed. Their efforts have been blunted. But they are in the process of regrouping for new attacks. And often the attacks are presented as reforms which cover up the ultra-reactionary substance. This is the case with S-1, the "electoral reform," and the Rockefeller CIA report. It is in the context of this reality that we must see the danger of fascism.

The debate as to whether we face the danger of fascism or not in the abstract has very little meaning. The fact is that in this stage in the development of monopoly capitalism the danger is inherent and always present. What we must see is the danger as it is represented in specific movements, specific programs, individuals and issues, as they appear today.

Fascism

Fascism is the open dictatorship of the most reactionary section of monopoly capital. That of course is a true statement. But to stop with a correct definition and not do anything about the fascist danger means to have illusions that it cannot happen in a country with 200 years of democratic experience or, on the other hand, that it is an inevitable stage of struggle. Of course, both assumptions are wrong. We must see that our activities may be the decisive factor in deciding the outcome. We must use the 200 years of experience in the struggle for democracy, but we cannot depend on it to block fascism. The struggle against today's reaction is the most effective struggle against fascism.

We must keep a sharp eye on how, in the U.S. in the 1970's, monopoly capital is preparing the political and ideological soil and the climate in which fascism can come to power.

We must keep an eye on how it is preparing a mass base which is one of the basic conditions for its victory. We must be alert to what issues are being used and what forces are moving into position. To fight fascism is to expose the meaning of these developments. Through the struggle we have the task of raising to higher levels the anti-fascist consciousness of the people. And there are individuals on the scene today who fit into this mold—the George Wallaces, General Westmorelands, Barry Goldwaters, the KKK and the Trotskyite-CIA-FBI-instigated Labor Caucus groups. The political mass base is in the ranks of the declassed, the petty-bourgeois elements, the police departments, including the laid-off ones.

The ideological currents that can be inflamed and generated by reaction to serve the fascist trend are great power chauvinism and the reactions to the Mayaguez action. Goldwater's statement about "those half-assed countries" is an example of how it can be used.

Racism serves as an ideological pillar, the mobilizing point for the forces of fascism. Therefore, any air of complacency about the fight against racism must be dispersed. This is clear from the ability of reaction to whip up an atmosphere of hysteria in Boston, and how the issue of busing generally has been used. It is also clear from how racism sustains an extremely repressive situation in North Carolina and other states. To fight the danger of fascism in the future is to fight against racism today.

We must be concerned about the fact that Wallace gets support with the demagogic line that he is the champion of "middle America," "the middle man" who is being squeezed and taxed to death by "big government, big monopolies and big trade unions." This is clearly an approach that prepares the soil, the atmosphere and the mass base for a potential fascist development. This "middle America" theme is connected to a campaign against social welfare and against so-called "excessive wages" which are both racist and anti-working class.

We should not be surprised that these ultra-right reactionary forces take up legitimate issues that are bothering the people, because demagogy is the main instrument of reaction as it is with fascism. Wallace wants to appear as, and calls himself, a "Populist"—again with the aim of building a mass base.

We are interested in the struggle against the evils of capitalism because we are interested in the welfare of the people.

But these same struggles serve the purpose of undermining and making it difficult for the demagogues to use the frustrations of the people for reactionary purposes.

Anti-communism is the deepest political and ideological expression of antagonism to the working class. Anti-communism is a weapon in the preparation of the soil and the atmosphere for fascism. There is a profound lesson about the use of anti-communism in the recent exposés of the FBI and CIA.

Anti-communism is the narcotic and the opium that tranquilized people, including most liberals and some on the left, into accepting the dirty work of the FBI and CIA and the anti-Communist laws "because they were directed against Communists." They were acceptable as long as it was the Communists who were imprisoned, fired and harassed. These anti-democratic processes were acceptable because they were initially said to be anti-Communist tools. Now the results of that drugging are being revealed.

It is true that these activities were and remain anti-Communist. But the sweep of their activities has reached far beyond the Communists. Murder, assassinations, the use of LSD, provocations, and now the total computerization of a blanket coverage of snooping. At the press of a button the authorities in Washington can have a dossier on any individual within seconds. Originally this was supposed to be limited to Communists. Now it involves the majority of the people. This computerized surveillance is a serious problem and violates the democratic rights of the people. But it also adds a new dimension to the danger of fascism.

We must warn against any move by monopoly capital to enact additional anti-labor legislation, the corporations' plans for strike-breaking and union-busting and their efforts to render unions ineffective in the class struggle. This calls for more attention to the class consciousness of workers, to the class struggle policies of the unions, and to recognizing in life the necessary and leading role of the working class in the united anti-fascist struggle.

To fight the danger of fascism means to expose the processes going on now, to expose the preparations of the soil and the atmosphere.

To build an anti-fascist unity is to build a unity in the struggle against the monopolies, and for the solution to the issues these reactionary forces demagogically use now.

We must inject an anti-fascist consciousness into all mass currents.

I have gone into some length on this question not because I think fascism is inevitable or that its coming to power is imminent. I think in this stage of developments we have to take a longer view of this danger and see its fibers in the fabric of today's reality. In so doing we can be an even bigger factor in determining the outcome of the struggle in such a way that it will never happen in the United States.

In times of great upsurge it is necessary to see the two sides of the dialectical process. The main tendency is that the forces of reaction and fascism are losing ground throughout the political globe. But there is no basis for complacency because as shadows follow substance, so danger stalks at the heels of new advances on the road of the new opportunities.

An army on the offensive must remain vigilant. We can have confidence in our struggle against reaction, but we can never be complacent.

So what is in the cards for the United States in the coming period? Serious economic problems, both short-term and long-term; continuing setbacks on the world scene; efforts of monopoly capital to cut down on the standard of living; further developments of state monopoly capitalism; drives to increase labor productivity; increased efforts to use and spread racism; continuing high military budgets; efforts by the Ford Administration to complete Nixon's efforts to destroy the social welfare system; new spurts of inflation; higher taxes and unemployment; more periodic layoffs and general economic and political instability. This will lead to a sharpening of all contradictions, especially the main class contradiction. This will continue to place the economic question in the very center of all struggles. This will obviously lead to a growth of mass militancy, to mass actions. It will further stimulate the process of radicalization. The words "tranquility and stabilization" do not appear in the cue cards.

5. MASS MOVEMENTS

The Main Political Resolution to this Convention goes into some detail on the nature of and the problems in the different mass movements. Also, the workshops which started their work yesterday are taking up these questions. They will report their findings and conclusions to this Convention later.

Therefore, I don't think it is necessary for this report to take up the same questions. So I will go into some questions that, to one extent or another, are similar and are reflected in all of the mass movements.

During past periods it was possible to think in terms of the ebb and flow of mass movements resulting in moments of relative inaction, when masses were not in motion. Such patterns reflected the slower tempo of developments. This is not the case today. And those who expect long periods of slack after a period of upsurge fall into patterns of waiting and routinism. Those are concepts from another period. The very nature of the present stage of developments dictates mass patterns of struggle that are more continuous. The issues triggering the upsurge and the fields of struggle may shift, but the patterns of mass upsurge are more constant. The mass reactions take on more crisis features.

The events of the past years have had a stimulating effect on the process of radicalization which affects all movements. But this has been especially so in the ranks of the working class. Masses are ready to accept and to fight for more radical solutions. For example, there has been a qualitative change in how broad sections of the people now view the prospects of nationalization. When we first raised the issue of nationalizing the energy complex it was looked upon as a far out idea, including by some of our own folks. Now the idea of nationalization, especially of the energy complex, is seriously being considered and weighed positively by the majority of the people, and again especially by workers. There is developing a mass anti-monopoly, anti-trust sentiment. It is a rising current within all of the mass movements. Because of this the possibilities for the development of the anti-monopoly coalition are much greater. The anti-military and peace sentiment is at an all-time high level at the present time. This comes through in all the opinion polls. It came through in response to the conferences against the high military budget.

A more conscious anti-imperialist sentiment is also at an unprecedented high level. The movements and the struggles against U.S. aggression in Indochina have had a deep influence on the thought patterns of millions. Because of Watergate and the accompanying exposés, the democratic sentiment, the sense of being on the alert and the awareness of the dangers to the democratic rights and institutions that most in the past took for granted have been significantly heightened.

The ruling class has many weapons that it uses to keep masses passive, and if not passive then divided. The opium of passivity is the ideological line that capitalism is the best of all systems, even with some shortcomings, and anyway it is now a people's capitalism that has done away with monopoly control. As the president of General Motors recently said, "Free enterprise is a cooperative system, not a class struggle," and "economic freedom is indivisible from our other freedoms." And they say that while capitalism used to come up with economic crises, it has now overcome the boom and bust cycle. And instead of using the old "one happy family" bromide, they now say, "We must all stick together because our country is in difficulties." This is the opium of passivity. And, while it is clear to us, this ideological propaganda line does have its effects. It is an obstacle on the path of struggle and radicalization.

But the main drug for the divide-and-rule policies of capitalism is racism. The drug of racism does not now have quite the same effect, but it remains the central obstacle to unity. There is the dialectical process—as monopoly capital gets into greater difficulties the pressures of the tendency to move towards a more reactionary position leading to repression becomes ever greater. The movement toward more reactionary positions in the first place includes an increase of racism. When capitalism is in difficulty, the weapon that divides movements and people becomes more important. There is evidence of this in all areas of life.

On the other hand, the pressures of the crisis and the sharpening contradictions, the attacks on the standard of living, the repression and the new dangers to democratic rights, generate movements and struggles and force the question of unity, which is the basic weapon of mass struggles, as an absolute necessity. So you have the two tendencies toward two directions.

An increase in racist oppression compels all progressives to make the struggle against racism an urgent matter in all of the movements.

It is necessary to take full advantage of the situation that the objective developments have created to burn out the influence of racism. We must master the arts of using the self-interest of white masses and their growing realization of the need for unity as a starting point in cleansing their minds of the racist fog.

Thus we should show that Ford and those who opose busing are exactly the people who cut funds for education, lay off teachers, and stand in the doorways of schools as barriers to integrated quality education. On the other hand, those who are for busing are those who are for more teachers, better schools and education, and for appropriations to meet all those needs. The educational system—from the nursery school to the graduate schools—can and must be a source of strength in the struggle against racism. This calls for the elimination of racism in the educational system and an organized program for the schools to fight racism in the country.

This must proceed simultaneously with a more basic attack on racism, its class roots and its incompatibility with any decent moral or ethical values or concepts of human decency.

This is a struggle that cannot be left for some future date. It must, of necessity, be an integrated, but a special feature of the building of unity, the building of movements and struggles, because victory or defeat depends on it. We must also reject any concept that at this stage we will gear the struggle to the self-interest of white masses and that at some other time we will raise it to a higher level. Such a concept will result in no struggle against racism. There is no such thing as struggling for the real self-interest of white workers without the struggle against racism.

We must keep hammering away and explaining that any victory against monopoly capital in the U.S. dictates a broad coalition that is based on an alliance of the working class with the peoples who are the victims of racist oppression—with Black, Puerto Rican, Asian and Native American peoples. We must keep explaining over and over again that the main stumbling block to such class unity and alliance is the influence of racism and the weaknesses in the struggle against racism by white Americans. We must take every positive step forward in the struggle against racism and build on it.

6. THE WORKING CLASS

In the center of all contradictions lies the basic class contradiction. In the center of all struggles is the class struggle. And in the center of all mass movements is the working class movement. That is the format and the lineup of forces in the struggle against monopoly capitalism. It is an essential element related to and affecting all mass movements. What is new in the arena of mass movements and the mass upsurge in the U.S. is that this basic class format has come into clearer focus, and the lineup is being restructured accordingly. To be sure, this same thing is taking place on different levels on a world scale. The working class is moving more forcefully to assume the leading role history has assigned to it.

Corresponding to the level of developments in the U.S. our working class is in step with this historic trend.

During this past crisis year it has been the working class front that has been the most active. Strikes have continued on a high level. Most of the initiatives, most of the participants in the mass actions around the economic questions have come from the shops and from the trade union movement. The main source of the stimulation for struggle has come from the organized rank and file movements. But there is a broad, deep ferment in the rank and file base of the working class that keeps surfacing and influencing events.

What is also new is that significant sections of the trade union leadership have responded to the pressures of the crisis and the membership, and have joined the ranks in struggle. In all of these developments Black workers, both on rank and file and leadership levels, as well as Chicano and Puerto Rican workers, have made some very special contributions.

The new trends in the trade union movement are best expressed in the movement ousting the Abel-Germano machine and the election of Sadlowski as President of the Gary-Chicago District 31 of the United Steelworkers. These new trends are expressed in the movement and struggles of the copper workers in the Southwest, in the economic and political struggles of the United Farm Workers. In both of these areas the Chicano workers are the base and therefore make special contributions.

The new trends are expressed in the turnover of the leadership of the coal miners union from the gangster, class collaborationist racist Boyle to a leadership more in tune with the interests of the coal miners.

These new trends are expressed in the mass demonstrations around problems of unemployment and especially in the tremendously significant mass demonstration on April 26th in Washington, D.C.

The new trends are expressed in the growth of an anti-Meany movement on all levels of the trade unions, membership and leadership. A small but a most significant indication of these new trends was the sit-in takeover of the Anaconda Copper Works in a small town in Westchester County, New York. Not only did the workers sit in, but the whole community was involved in a struggle against the closing of the plant. It has turned into a significant anti-monopoly action. This is a strong indication of the mood and the developing level of the working class movement. The new trends are set in the growing Black-white unity of the working class in the South.

The new trends are reflections of the fact that the working class is not passively accepting the corporate policy of making the workers pay for the crisis. The working class is not passively accepting the drive to cut the standard of living. These developments in the ranks of the working class are the most significant and meaningful barometer of the nature of the weather now showing up on the economic and political radar screen.

The new winds are present in the isolation of the Meany leadership from the world trade union movement and the growing ties that are developing with the World Federation of Trade Unions and with the various unions of workers working for the same multi-national corporations.

In all of this, the source, the spark, and very often the lead for direction comes from the organized rank and file movements. In a sense they set the standards of militancy. They give the movements a sense of politics. They spearhead the struggles on ideological issues. They have carried the struggle against racism and for political independence to new levels.

And in all this the Trade Unionists for Action and Democracy (TUAD) and *Labor Today* continue making significant contributions as centers and as a voice of the movements for class struggle trade unionism. They do this by stimulating struggles, organization, and thought. TUAD has the additional responsibility of becoming an initiator and stimulator for a broader trade union unity, involving the section of the leadership cadre that is ready to step out of the old patterns.

Meanyism continues to be the main obstacle to a viable class struggle trade union movement. Under pressure, even the Meanys make public statements protesting corporate and government actions. But statements of protest without the organization of struggle only serve as a cover for policies of class collaboration. Statements against racism while condoning it in industry and in the unions are a cover for racism. What we are seeing are the beginnings of an important shift to policies of struggle that are pushing class collaboration to the ropes. Even the love feast between Alexander Solzhenitsyn and George Meany will not help.

The growth of class consciousness, the struggle against class collaboration, the need to organize rank and file groups, the struggle against racism, the struggle for working class and trade union unity, the concept of class struggle trade unionism, and Communist shop work are all parts of a very closely integrated, non-contradictory task, referred to as industrial concentration. Each part adds and draws strength from the others. They are not a list of separate tasks. It is this integrated task that is the centerpiece for the Party's trade union and shop work.

I want to briefly deal with some of the problems as they relate to the key struggles for working class and trade union unity.

As we so well know, the struggle for unity is a basic requirement. We Communists must at all times be the most active, the most consistent force for class unity. In our specific situation it is the organized rank and file that is creating the foundation for unity. Therefore, we must continue to give our full support to the organization of rank and file groups. In this work we must get away from an approach that is stiff, stereotyped, bookish, and unimaginative in relation to forms, issues and the levels of the rank and file groups.

A rank and file group does not have to be antagonistic to workers who are elected to union leadership. Rank and file leaders who are elected to office, as they should be, must not allow themselves to be separated from their rank and file base.

A rank and file group can be organized around one issue or a number of issues. It can be of center forces or it can be of the left, or it can be some center and left. It can be non-public or it can be open. They may or they may not have relationships with existing national forms. They can be recognized as part of the union structure, as caucuses, or they can operate as independent forms.

The rank and file forms can be varied and versatile as are the situations in the shops and in the unions. But in all situations, we must as much as possible, make them into a force for more advanced concepts, for militancy, for class and trade union unity. They can be training grounds for a new breed of trade union leader, a force against class collaboration and racism.

In order to give this broad development some national and state coordination it is obvious that TUAD centers and *Labor Today* are essential instruments in this struggle.

Based on past experience I think it is necessary to see the rank and file movements as key factors in the struggle for Black-white unity—the unity of a multi-national (Black, Chicano, Puerto Rican, Native and Asian American and white) working class. In the past period, no matter what the original form of a rank and file group has been, this is the direction to which they have all gravitated. They have all tended to become multi-national.

Therefore, beside all other specific issues or reasons for organizing rank and file groups, we should take the initiative to organize them for the specific purpose of a struggle for class unity based on the fight against racism and chauvinism. They should serve as caucuses in the struggle for the multinational unity of the local or international unions. When they cannot convince the unions to do so, such groups can organize their own educational campaign.

A central task for such caucuses today would be the struggle against the racist patterns of the crisis layoffs. There are some tendencies to speak about the contradiction between preserving the established seniority systems and the racist patterns of the layoffs, but to do nothing about this problem. In practice, this kind of behavior is support for the continuation of the racist cycle of last-to-be-hired and first-to-be-fired. In these situations the monopolies, with great glee, are saying: "We are neutral. We will do whatever you say. Fight it out among yourselves."

We must work to build a force that presents and puts the issue squarely—that it is a class issue but that it is affected by the generations of corporate policies of racial discrimination. The struggle must be raised in the framework of no layoffs and jobs for all. But this framework must not become a framework for general talks about no layoffs and jobs for all, while doing nothing about the racist layoffs that are going on. The struggle must get to the specifics of breaking the racist cycle. It must get to the specifics of special adjustments and of preferential hiring and layoffs. Once white workers are convinced of the necessity of these special adjustments there are concrete ways in which they can be carried out.

For example, the Labor Research Association, in its *Economic Notes*, presents an idea. The idea comes from trade union leaders with a long history of struggle:

> Instead of laying off the younger workers, where the minorities are concentrated, the older workers would be furloughed. They would be paid 95% of their working wages and continue to receive Social Security and pension credits, and also be fully covered by the existing medical plan. When the economy picked up, they would return to their jobs.
>
> This would stretch out the life span of the older workers and strengthen the unions by gaining the support of the younger workers. It would also promote union solidarity because it would end discriminatory layoffs.
>
> The furloughed workers would receive their wages from state unemployment funds plus a federal supplement, including upward adjustments when wages are raised. There would be no time limits on these payments and no need for bi-weekly reports, only on initial registration.

The struggle against racism must be worked into concrete demands and concrete plans of struggle. And it must be placed within the context of the fight for working class and trade union unity. Then it can be concretely related to the self-interests of all workers.

In these last years, there have been some important legal victories that have helped in the struggle against racism such as the Fairfield decision. It is important to use such victories in every way possible. They have created cracks in the wall of racism.

However, as is the case with all partial victories, especially when they come from the courts, and even more so when they do not specifically strike at the roots of the system of racism, or when they only apply to individuals or groups of individuals, we must be careful that we expose the limitations of such measures. Otherwise it leads to illusions that the struggle against racism has been won, and therefore the struggle can cease.

Our Party has for some time placed special emphasis on our work in the working class and trade union sector. We will and we should be self-critical about many of the weaknesses in our policy of industrial concentration. But it is also necessary to draw the positive lessons. We are now seeing the beginning of a new period. Because of our working class emphasis during the past years, we are on the ground floor of this upswing. Because of it we are an integral part of this important development.

Women Workers

It is from the same viewpoint of the struggle for working-class unity that we must now take up, in a new way, the questions around discrimination against women workers. There can be no talk of class or trade union unity without seriously taking up the struggle for the full equality of workers who are women.

A few facts should convince anyone of this. Over 40% of the paid work force in the U.S. are now women. And the percentage continues to increase. The dramatic nature of the change can be seen in the developments of the last ten years. Of the 17 million additional jobs that were added to the total labor force in the last ten years, 10 million of these 17 million have been filled by women workers. There are 13 million working mothers. Four and a half million of the working class women are of the racially oppressed national groups. There are no difficulties in documenting the discrimination against women workers. The wages of women workers continue to average about 60% of what the wages of male workers are. And this gap has not gotten smaller. The larger the number of women workers being paid 60% of the wages of males, the higher the corporate profits. As in the case with the racist patterns of the crisis layoffs, there is a pattern of firing a disproportionate number of women workers who have a lower standing on the seniority lists.

With the passage of the Equal Rights Amendment by states the corporations have already in many cases eliminated, and now ignore, measures and regulations that provided some protection which helped make it possible to fight for full equality of women workers. Most union leaders still either ignore the problems of women workers or continue to treat them as if they were going to be in industry for a short period, or as if they were members of the union's "women's auxiliary."

The controversy over the Equal Rights Amendment (ERA) continues—including in the ranks of our Party. Why there is controversy is clear. Because there is a contradiction to which we have not yet found a solution. We must recognize this fact. What is the contradiction? That the overall sense of equality contained in the Equal Rights Amendment to the Constitution is in conflict with existing state and city measures that provide some sense of protection for women workers in industry. As a working class party our focus is on the women who are workers.

No one in our Party can seriously argue that our Party does not have a basic and a principled position for the full equality of women. It is slander to argue otherwise. In fact, it is because of our principled position on equality that we have been critical of the ERA.

In order to know what the problems are let us place on the table some basics. There is a need for special laws and regulations for the protection of women workers in industry and especially in the basic industries. Only those who have never been in basic industry can argue otherwise. Wherever there has been a strong trade union movement such laws were passed. The ERA is an amendment to the U.S. Constitution. It specifically and directly supercedes all such laws. But it is a more difficult matter. Attorneys argue that because the ERA is an amendment to the Constitution, it becomes a constitutional bar to all such laws in the future. They will be ruled out as unconstitutional.

The National Commission for the Equality of Women has worked out and projected the Women's Bill of Rights. It overcomes the flaws in ERA. So some say, let's get the ERA passed and then we will fight for the Women's Bill of Rights. But if the attorneys are right, the Equal Rights Amendment will be the constitutional bar to such a bill.

Some argue that we supported the Civil Rights Act. That is correct. But there are at least two differences. One, it is not an amendment to the constitution; and secondly, it did not wipe out any local laws against racism.

Some in the pre-convention discussion have argued that if we do not support the ERA we will be isolated. That is a poor argument, first because it is not true. Wherever the Women's Bill of Rights has been presented we have not been isolated. And even if it was partially true, it's a poor argument. We cannot opportunistically go along with a proposition because it is popular.

So, one, we have a contradiction. Two, we do not have all of the facts on all of the ramifications—legal as well as practical. So we mean to propose the only possible solution at this time— that this Convention instruct the incoming Central Committee to set up a study task force that will go fully into all sides of the question and try to come up with a resolution that takes all questions into consideration.

From the reports so far it seems the International Women's Year is making a historic contribution the world over. We greet the World Conference on Women sponsored by the United Nations in Mexico City. Its constructive decisions need to be implemented.

The question of the discrimination against women workers is an old problem, but now it has a new dimension. It is now an important feature of the class question. And in many ways, of key significance is the role of the 5 million working class women who are exploited as workers, discriminated against because they are women and are the victims of racist oppression. They are a key link within the class and within the lineup of the people's formations of struggle. The struggle against discrimination practiced against women workers must be placed within the context of a developing class consciousness and a unified working class.

A starting point can be the self-interest of the class, including the self-interest of the male workers.

The emergence of CLUW as a coalition of labor union women, was a response to the new role and the problems of women workers. This is a question the rank and file movement must take up seriously, as a special question.

What should also become clearly evident is that the problems of these working class women must be the focal point of the overall struggle for equality of women. From all this it should also be self-evident why there is a real need for the organization of Women for Racial and Economic Equality (WREE).

Young Workers

In this period of upsurge young workers are playing a very important role in most of the rank and file movements and in the struggles against racism. They are giving all of the movements a new sense of militancy.

Starting with ourselves, but following through, we must give a lead to the trade union movement, the rank and file groups, for a basic change in the attitudes and approach to young workers. Young workers have special problems that must be dealt with. This is also a necessary ingredient of working class unity. Young workers can and do make a very unique and special contribution to the whole class.

The process of radicalization that had its beginning earlier very quickly acquires a working class content once young workers enter the ranks of the exploited.

The crisis layoffs from the young end of seniority have sharply brought to the fore new problems and have especially raised the questions of jobs and job security. The sudden loss of a job, and the realization that there is no job security, has been a great shock to millions of young workers. These are problems that the trade union movement must respond to.

There can be no unity if there is an age gap. The problems of trade union democracy are a special issue for all newer workers. Beside the general problems of a bureaucratic structure, there is the problem that most leadership posts are held by older white men. This is a special problem for the rank and file groups. They must make special efforts to include in their leadership and membership the sections that are kept out of union leadership posts. The struggle for trade union democracy must include the fight to break up the older, white male, and in many cases, skilled workers' domination of union leadership posts. In mass production industries the leadership should come from the the ranks of the basic workers. Like the working class, the leadership must be multi-national, of both sexes and both young and old.

Leadership Cadre

Our correct emphasis on the building of rank and file movements must continue. But, as in all cases, this emphasis must not limit or narrow our approach to the point where we ignore changes that are taking place in the leadership cadre of the trade union movement.

There are important changes in leadership positions, especially on the middle and lower levels. We must take note of the anti-Meany sentiment that is emerging. The anti-Meany sentiment is a movement against Meany's politics and the sellout policies of class collaboration. This trend includes important center and left forces. We see this as an important break with the past.

We extend a hand of welcome and cooperation to all who want

to become involved in one way or another in the movements and struggles of our class. The rank and file movements can continue to grow, they will be the source of stimulation, and in many cases the source for direction. But they must now, in one way or another, relate to and reflect the broader movements that are in motion. Because of this their task is even greater. We must work with and encourage the new realignment that is taking place. The realignment is moving in the direction of the emergence of a new left-center that reflects the forces of today's developments.

Related to the development of a left-center current are questions of the working class relations with other sectors of the population. We must do more to explain and to convince the trade union movement of the necessity, in its own class interest and as a part of its leading role, of the need to establish coalition relationships in the first place with the racially oppressed people, but also with all who are victims of monopoly oppression. And for ourselves we must add that our emphasis on the working class in no way can be an obstacle to paying attention to the full scope of the struggles and movements. Our class emphasis is not a narrow emphasis limited solely to the working class.

On the economic front—and no matter when the crisis is bottoming out—the fight for a shorter work week will emerge as a key demand. It affects all of the areas we have discussed. The demand for a 30-hour week with a 40-hour wage is realistic *and* necessary.

Electoral Scene

The politics of the country are now being drawn into the orbit of the 1976 presidential elections. In spite of all the phony rhetoric that accompanies bourgeois electoral campaigns and the severe limitations of the electoral process under monopoly capital, the months of the presidential elections are the liveliest, the most intense period of mass political involvement. From now till the elections tens of millions will be thinking politically. They are seeking political solutions to the serious problems the people face.

The elections take on added significance because all movements and struggles are taking on a political aspect. It is truly a great challenge and a tremendous opportunity.

The political struggles are becoming increasingly decisive in all matters—in matters of jobs, inflation, taxation, welfare, police brutality, racism, detente, peace, militarism, actions by the CIA and the FBI in the undermining of democracy and the developments toward a police state. The political aspects of all struggles naturally relate to electoral politics.

The challenge is how to help crystallize a popular, anti-monopoly alternative, a common-front alternative to the two parties of monopoly capital; how to unite the broad forces who are disillusioned with the two old parties, with the people who have not yet fully cut their political apron-strings. The challenge is how to build the basis for political independence; how to convince, how to bring these disillusioned but radicalized masses into the electoral activities. The challenge is how our Party can speak to and influence the thinking patterns of tens of millions.

In short, how can our Party become a factor in the great national debate of 1976? How can we influence the outcome of the elections?

In spite of the increasing activities the electoral scene is still very unsettled. But there are many new factors that we must consider.

The percentage of people who do not identify with or support either of the two old parties is now the largest in history. Also, the number of voters who do not vote is at an all-time high. It is estimated that some 75% of the eligible voters, those who do not register, and those who register but do not vote, are not in the electoral process. Most elections are won with a majority of the 25% who do vote. Also, voters who consider themselves independents are now the largest single political grouping.

It is the largest, but it has no organized centers, programs, or leadership. Much of this spells disillusionment with politics as they have been; frustration because there is no viable alternative; and confusion because there is no clear lead. But it also indicates a tremendous veering away from, and rejection of, politics as usual.

Both of the parties have their ordinary run-of-the-mill reactionaries and the ultra-right reactionaries. In both cases the aim of the ultra-right forces is to push their party toward their ultra-right position. And in both cases they are having some successes.

At this moment it looks like both parties will have right-of-center presidential slates. The liberal forces tend to be dispersed and to this point are more than ever playing the game of "who is the lesser of two evils." This is increasingly becoming a difficult row to hoe when both are becoming more evil. But as the anti-monopoly sentiment grows, the possibilities for an independent political alternative also grow. Therefore, the possibilities for the organization of an independent political alternative are much greater now than they were four years ago, or two years ago.

To be meaningful, the alternative must encompass the broad sections of people who feel they cannot get a hearing, or find solutions to their grievances within the limitations of the two-party system. It must encompass the trade unionists who feel the boot of monopoly capital and who have given up on the two old parties and are seeking for ways to register the working class self-interest through the elections. It must encompass the numerous electoral movements reflecting the Black community, including the Black Congressional Caucus, and the Black trade union leadership movement. This alternative must be of such a nature, that it is possible for political leaders and elected officials to support the broad alternative, and still not have to cut their ties with the party forces that helped to get them elected.

This alternative must encompass the broad Chicano and Puerto Rican movements. It must encompass the varied movements fighting for the equality of women and a broad sweep of the youth movements. It must encompass the peace forces, people's neighborhood organizations, and the movements fighting for civil liberties.

As a Party we are going to call on all progressives, independents, and anti-monopoly forces to join in a dialogue now on how to best put forward a people's alternative, a common electoral front against the monarchs of monopoly capital, against the Fords, Rockefellers, Jacksons and Wallaces.

We also urge an all-out campaign for working class candidates for public office from the shops and unions, the Blacks, Puerto Ricans and the oppressed masses, from the mass organizations and mass struggles. The chief steward and local union official, and many in the higher ranks of labor tested in the class struggle and in the fight against racism, are worthy of high political office. Many from the Black liberation movement, Chicano and Puerto Rican struggles, women and youth with responsibility in struggle for social progress can change the nature of government bodies.

Yes, there is a multitude of potential working class candidates who will serve the needs of the people instead of the profit of the monarchs of monopoly capital. A lot of present and recent public office-holders are bloated with money but politically bankrupt. They are arrogant, cruel, brutal, parasitic, racist and corrupt. That adds to the necessity for working class candidates for public office. Such candidates will give a new quality to the elections, to public officials, and to democracy. In fact, there will not be a qualitative change in the present electoral picture until there is a change in the class composition of the candidates, reflecting a new class base for mass politics.

As the anti-monopoly struggles continue to involve ever greater masses, and as the people's coalitions and working class struggles develop for the needs of the people in this period of depression and crisis, the two parties of monopoly are demonstrating their political bankruptcy. They become ever more exposed as having no serious concern for the people. The masses in struggle are moving into the beginning stage of a new mass anti-monopoly political party to challenge the two-party set-up.

Such a mass party can develop from a mass working-class base, in coalition with other sections of the population in mass struggles against racism and repression, and for a new standard and people's content in democracy. It will aid the struggle for detente and a peace policy by slashing the military budget to meet the needs of the people in the fight for jobs and decent living standards. It would be a force against reaction, the ultra-right and fascism. Such a mass electoral party perspective is essential.

And, even if we became convinced that it is not viable for 1976, we must continue to work for it. Such a party is on the agenda for the mass of people and the future of the country.

As Communists we will make our contributions on two fronts of the same struggle. We will take initiatives, work with other forces, give our full support for the crystallization of the broad electoral alternative. And we will make a contribution by fighting to put the Communist Party on the ballot in all of the 50 states. We will make a contribution by filing local and presidential candidates. To be able to do this we must continue to challenge the restrictions against Communists and all progressive candidates that are still on the books in most states.

In the last few years we have made considerable progress in our Party electoral work. We have fought our way from the status of not having our votes counted to 2% of the vote, to 5%, to 15% and (already) with the vote for Comrade Mark Allen, to 35%. And we have now capped this with the significant victorious break-through election of our Comrade Alva Buxenbaum to the district school board in Brooklyn, New York, and the election of Amadeo Richardson to the Anti-Poverty Board in Chelsea, New York. This is important progress.

We must continue this line of march. We should still run Communist candidates who we know will not get elected. But we must now pick candidates in areas with the aim of electing Communists to office. We must have a plan for building winning Communist people's candidates, a plan that includes becoming known as fighters for the interests of the people supported by broad coalitions.

Together with others, we will hold an electoral campaign and presidential nominating convention in the early part of next year. And then, we will organize the most massive political, ideological and electoral campaign in our Party's history.

Anti-Monopoly Struggle

More than any other single factor, the one that completely dominates and engulfs life in the U.S. is the unlimited power, both economic and political, that is exercised by the ruling monarchs of monopoly capital. They totally dominate the economy and they have absolute control of the decision-making bodies of the state. Their economic domination is symbolized by the fact that in most every major line of production, including agriculture and food, there are only three corporations that control it. Sixty-five per cent of all manufacturing sales come from such 3-corporate industries. Less than 200 manufacturing companies now control 63% of all manufacturing assets.

In some cases, two or all three are owned by the same financial interests. An example of the political control is Nelson Rockefeller as head of the Rockefeller family empire and as vice president of the United States, and their paid family servant, the Secretary of State. The monarchs of monopoly capital control the executive branch, the National Security Council, CIA, FBI, the Judiciary (including the Supreme Court), a majority of Congress, and most state and city governments.

The new developments of state monopoly capitalism have

given the top dogs of monopoly literally dictatorial power without precedent in U.S. history. During his coronation, Rockefeller
said: "There is no conflict of interest," in his position as Vice
President. From the viewpoint of the monarchs of monopoly
capital he is right. There is no conflict of interest. It is completely in their interests. But the unlimited power, the tyranny
of top monopoly circles, is now in ever sharper conflict with
the interest of the great majority of people, and in ever sharper
conflict with the interest of the nation. This greatly sharpened
contradiction has emerged as a focal center for all issues and
struggles. It is generating a deep and militant anti-monopoly
sentiment.

There can be no meaningful mass movements that ignore
this hard core of our reality. For our Party, the anti-monopoly struggle must now become the target center for our
strategic and tactical considerations. We must burn out all
leftovers of past influences of petty-bourgeois, radical idiocy;
ideas that somehow the anti-monopoly struggle is a phase we
are going to skip over in the U.S. Or, the concept that it is not
important because it is not a struggle against capitalism. We
must also reject all ideas that the anti-monopoly struggle is a
generalized, abstract concept without form or without a concrete
program. Such concepts lead to spontaneity, to a game of waiting.

The anti-monopoly concept is not an invention. It is the
only realistic, winning response to the reality of monopoly domination. It is not a diversion. It is the only realistic path along
which masses will move in the struggle for the elimination of
capitalism. Even more, it is the path they are now moving along.
It is not something we have to invent or create. The sharp edge
of the struggle must be directed against the monarchs of monopoly capital, the top dominating section of monopoly capital.

It is this that gives a special meaning to the concept of
using divisions in the ranks of the ruling class.

The anti-monopoly outlook can give a focus to trade union

and working-class unity. It is a stimulant for class consciousness. It is an essential feature of the struggle against the ultra-right, against the danger of fascism. It gives a class focus to the struggle against racism. Above all, it provides the broadest framework for the democratic struggles. It provides the foundation for electoral programs and for coalitions of political independence.

The anti-monopoly concept can give anti-imperialism a deeper and broader base. The anti-monopoly struggle is the key in the struggle against monopoly capitalism. The anti-monopoly concept places the struggle for socialism not as something that is talked about, a good thing waiting in the wings of time, but instead, as a vibrant participant, an influence on the thought patterns, a subject debated and talked about as it relates to the struggles against monopoly, as an idea that grows with the experiences in the struggle against monopoly domination. Whether the issues are in the field of culture or ideology, the focal point is monopoly domination.

We must do much more in formulating a program and finding the forms for this movement. Of course we must not make the mistake of thinking that if we work out a blueprint that this will solve the problem. As it is now developing, the anti-monopoly sentiment does not take the form of only a one-organization or one-issue movement. At the present time, it is focused around unemployment, inflation and the crisis of services in the cities.

In working out and projecting programs it is necessary that the proposals are clearly directed against the top monopolies, because there are many people who are ready to support much more basic and radical solutions to their problems. Because of this it is necessary and possible now to think in terms of projecting programs and solutions that go beyond the traditional concepts of what are called bourgeois democratic levels.

The program for nationalization must have a sharp and clear anti-monopoly objective. That is one of the reasons why the idea of nationalizing the energy complex, the biggest of all ripoffs, receives such wide support. That is also the reason why we must work out and emphasize the methods of nationalization and democratic control of such nationalized facilities.

The struggle against militarization, the astronomical war budgets and war production must have a sharp anti-monopoly direction. We must pinpoint the monopoly circles who are the war profiteers. We have reached a new level, a new phase in the struggle against the awesome powers of the top monopoly circles.

The new level calls for new and bolder initiatives. It calls for bold injection of the anti-monopoly concept into all struggles and movements. It calls for bolder projection of concrete anti-monopoly measures and control, restrictions and take-over. It calls for bolder initiatives in calling for and organizing coalitions that are drawn together by the broad issues affecting the people because of the unlimited power of the monarchs of monopoly capital.

We must reject all sectarian approaches that hamstring us even before we get started. Our correct emphasis on the need for, and the strength that comes from, a basic alliance of the working class with the racially oppressed peoples, must not in any way limit our approach, or blind us from seeing the importance of other sectors that can be brought into broad anti-monopoly movements. As we move with the movements and struggles we will, of course, have to be vigilant about right opportunistic pressures. We will be able to fight them best while we are actively giving leadership to broad movements.

From all this it should be self-evident why our Party must give a new priority to this important question. We should take the initiative to organize a broad consultative conference to work out an anti-monopoly program and anti-monopoly movement.

United Front

I want to express some thoughts on our approach to a question that is termed "our policy of united front." I am using the term here as Lenin used it to describe the basic Communist approach, the method of mobilizing and uniting masses in struggle.

In this crisis period as movements and struggles rise to higher levels our attitude, approach and our Party's relationships to such movements become an ever more critical question. In a sense they determine whether we are a mass party. And it involves the basic question of how we fulfill the vanguard role of the Party. This applies to our efforts to unite the ranks of the working class that were discussed earlier in this report, as well as to our policies of unity in all sections of mass work.

Unity of struggle around specific issues is a fundamental approach and a structure for our mass work. A Party club that does not work to build a movement or movements of people united on the basis of specific issues is a Party club living in sectarian isolation.

There are no real problems in unifying the people who agree with us on all questions (although sometimes I wonder). The task is to unify and to unite with masses who do not see eye to eye with us on many questions. The overall aim of all efforts of unity must be to move masses into actions and struggles. Therefore, we are for the unity of all honest forces who are interested in the issues and struggles which are collectively decided upon as the purpose of the unity.

Thus, it follows that in such movements it is not necessary to have or insist on having agreement on other questions, for example, on fundamental questions of doctrine, theory or ideological questions. Saying this we, of course, cannot put such questions into cold storage. But we also do not place them as a condition for unity, including unity with us Communists.

We will and we must continue to discuss and debate such

questions and all questions on which we may not agree with the non-Communist forces who are participating in the united movement. In carrying on such discussions and debates the aim must be to win honest masses who are still influenced by fake propaganda. We fight for the democratic character of all organizations and movements in which we participate. And we are for bringing the leading forces of the broader movement into the active leading committee of such movements.

In such united movements we do not and we need not insist that the non-Communists must recognize or accept the leading role of the Communists. Leadership questions should be settled on the basis of unity. As to who will contribute most with ideas and manpower, life and experience will decide. We have confidence such decisions will lean in our direction.

We must resist all sectarian pressures. We must keep the option open that as a result of experiences in movements and struggles people will change their attitudes. We must be flexible about ideas we may have as to forms or the levels of movements. They should be crystallized in the process of experience with others.

In the struggle for united movements, the objective basis for the broad appeal for unity lies in the fact that the great majority of the people are victims of monopoly capital. How to break the grip of monopoly capital has emerged as a critical daily question. Our perspective must encompass not just opposition movements but majority movements—winning the majority movements.

We must learn to swim in big ponds with turbulent waters. To learn to swim in big ponds means to swim but not get lost in the crowd, and not stay on the bank because of the danger of getting lost.

We must learn to swim in big ponds while pushing aside the debris and the weeds.

We have to make the appeal that says: "We disagree on many things. But if we do not unite against the enemy that is oppressing and exploiting all of us, we will lose even the opportunity to disagree."

We must learn to say: "Look, it does not matter what you call yourself—independent, Socialist, Liberal, Democrat or Republican. What counts is that we get together and fight for a program—a fight against big business economics, big business politics. What counts is that we are all being ground into the ground. It does not matter what you call yourself as long as you answer the call to unity."

We are for the broadest unity possible, keeping in mind that it is much easier to narrow the movement than it is to broaden it. This approach to the method of mobilizing masses is guided by our principled position on the basic question of the class struggle.

Because we are for the broadest unity we will fight against all elements who are in any way destructive. We will fight disruption whether it comes in a left or a right cover. We will fight all who in any way inject racism, both because it is wrong from the viewpoint of all human and moral standards and because it is disruptive of unity. We will fight all attempts at injecting or using anti-communism, both because it is false and a big lie, and because it is disruptive of unity. If there is one basic lesson from the cold war that we must not let anyone forget it is the disastrous consequences to the mass movements that flowed from the red-baiting and the exclusion of Communists from mass movements, including the trade unions. We must keep this lesson burning brightly.

We will fight any attempt to disrupt the unity on specific issues by faslesly and abstractly injecting concepts under the name of bringing in advanced ideas, or artificially setting the acceptance of socialism as a precondition for the unity. We will fight such disruption because it is not a struggle for socialism and it is and can be disruptive. This method of disruption has been the stock in trade of Trotskyites for over 50 years.

As new millions are forced to take the road of struggle, and as the process of radicalization continues because of monopoly capitalism's policies of exploitation and oppression, the potential base for united movements continues to broaden and grow. Our projection for united movements must of necessity take into account this growing scope of mass developments in this period.

This process prepares and forces greater numbers to think in terms of more basic solutions. The process of radicalization gives rise to a larger left political current. It is therefore necessary to consider and take initiatives for the organization of united left formations. We are not for such forms in the abstract.

Such formations are meaningful only when they are part of and operate as a guiding left force within the broader movements. This is true for the trade unions as well as other mass movements. It follows that such left forms can be viable when they accept the concept that building united mass movements is a method of mobilizing masses for struggle.

In greater numbers than has been the case—possibly at any other moment in our 55 years—masses are reaching the level of radicalization where they are ready to consider the alternative of socialism as a basic solution. In some of the opinion polls the indications are that there are tens of millions of such Americans.

Unfortunately, not all who reach this turn on the political and ideological path come into our Party. But we have the task of working to influence and to win over this sector. The greatest number of these socialist oriented masses are not a part of or related to any party or group. Therefore, we must take this development into consideration in our efforts to build united movements of struggle, especially in our initiatives at building left forms.

Both sections of the Social Democrats are actively engaged in trying to relate to or to use this new base. One of the sectors works to tie it to the tail end of the Democratic Party. The other uses it in their efforts to give Meany's policies of class collaboration a socialist, a radical hue.

Most Americans hailed the victories of the people in Vietnam, Laos, Cambodia. But the right-wing Socialists did not. In their publication they lamented, "For us, the Social-Democrats there is no relief in the Communist triumph in Indochina." "We have been dismayed by the American retreat—we have not been surprised at the recent turn of events. On the contrary, we have stated that the American policy of unconditional detente with the Soviet Unions would lead to unprecedented American setbacks." How sad! We want to be helpful but knowing that the setbacks for U.S. imperialism will continue we can only say, "cry your opportunistic hearts out." We must continue to expose such out and out policies based on right opportunism. But while doing so we must find ways to extend our hand in friendship and urge the people, and especially the youth, who want to take part in struggles around immediate issues, while continuing to study and probe the socialist alternative, to work with us and all those in the united mass movements.

We must recognize that there are differences among them. They are not of one mold, or of the same experiences in struggles. Many among them use Marxist-Leninist words loosely and without understanding. In this process, some will join us and we should welcome them and encourage them to bring others into better working relations and possibly join us. That will give greater strength and breadth to the united front movement.

In the process we will expose and reject the phonies who misuse Marxism-Leninism and discredit Marxism-Leninism. We must always make it clear that we are not an obstacle to the unity of all who see the future of the U.S. in terms of socialism.

As a Party, on all levels we must master the Leninist art of stimulating, swimming with and leading broad mass currents. We must master the method of organizing and leading mass movements. In the process our Party will emerge as a mass party and Communists will become even better mass leaders.

We Communists must see the dialectical relationship of mass struggles to the basic revolutionary process—of politically and ideologically preparing the forces for the overthrow of capitalism. Lenin correctly emphasized that in the "search for forms of the transition or *approach* to the proletarian revolution, propaganda and agitation alone are not enough for an entire class, the broad masses of the working people, those oppressed by capital to take up such a stand. *For that, the masses must have their own political experience.* Such is the fundamental law of all great revolutions."

7. THE PARTY

Since the last Convention, our Party has come a long way—in fact a hell of a long way.

Who can seriously challenge the fact that we are now the most viable, most influential, the fastest growing, the best organized, the most youthful, the liveliest, perkiest, and most united force on the left bank of U.S. politics. We have left the doubters and the skeptics, the left political sidewalk superintendents, the corporate ideologues and the soothsayers in the liberal camp somewhat baffled and confused. They are bewildered because we are the one organization only a few years ago some predicted would die, would wither on the political vine. Their predictions were that the Party would wither away because it was irrelevant, old; it had lost its revolutionary character mainly because it stuck to its positions of internationalism; because it continued with the old bag of classes and class struggle; because it did not join U.S. imperialism and its CIA-Voice of America anti-Soviet slander; and because it would not opportunistically set aside the struggle against racism. They are baffled because most of the organizations they predicted would replace the Communist Party are now in shambles, and the one organization they predicted would die is now the most relevant, viable and growing organization on the left.

For some, such predictions were calculated slander. For others, it was just simply miscalculation. The ones who miscalculated did not understand the laws of capitalist development, the basic nature of the class struggle, the role of classes, and our relationship to such developments. They did not understand the unique nature of our Party, they did not have the benefit of a revolutionary science, they did not understand that the Communist Party is not just another organization on the left— that Marxism-Leninism is not just another body of thought. It is a basic revolutionary science.

The Communist Party is relevant because it refuses to be swayed by opportunistic pressures, because it refuses to follow will-o-the-wisp, subjective fantasies. It is the Party with working-class principles. It doesn't compromise to the ruling class, and not to the publicity agents or media of that class. It has a working-class loyalty and is in the class struggle. Communists don't seek an easy, cheap buck from the book publishers. The Communist Party is unique.

We are here because we have our feet planted firmly in the soil of U.S. class realities. I really don't want to sound too boastful. It's just that the truth sometimes does sound that way.

And of course we do have weaknesses and shortcomings.

The basic class contradiction based on the capitalist law of private appropriation of the socially produced products continues to give rise to new problems which, in turn, propels new movements and new struggles. In all this, spontaneity to one extent or another may be a temporary factor. But in a basic sense, the potential of that which surfaces with the mass upsurge can be realized only by a conscious effort of organization and leadership.

Thus, capitalist relationships and the class struggle as a continuous process present situations that call for initiatives and leadership. With such initiatives vacuums develop—vacuums looking for initiatives and leadership. The political force that moves into such vacuums becomes the leading force. One of the reasons our Party has gained influence since our last Convention is that we have taken the initiatives, often together with others, in many areas where life has presented vacuums. This is true where we have been instrumental in organizing rank and file groups. The sharpening class contradiction and the class collaborationist leadership create vacuums and opportunities.

This is true regarding TUAD. It is the case with the organization of the National Alliance Against Racist and Political Repression. The latest examples of this initiative and moving into a vacuum is the movement which has resulted in the National Coalition to Fight Inflation and Unemployment. This is also true with the work of the National Anti-Imperialist Movement in Solidarity with African Liberation. Our Party's initiative plays an important role in the movement against the junta in Chile, in the struggle against the military budget and in many other areas. These are significant initiatives and examples of leadership.

However, I am sure you will not be surprised when I say that in spite of these examples we cannot be satisfied. We cannot be satisfied for many reasons. First, because life presents the vacuums as a continuous process. Therefore, we cannot rest on the laurels of our past initiatives. Second, because we do not always follow through (as they say in golf lingo). Third, because we do not always give the same attention in building the grass roots base for these movements. Fourth, because we have missed the bus in many cases.

For example, we have talked a lot about the economic questions. We all agree the problems facing the people are urgent and serious. Based on that sound judgment we took important initiatives in organizing movements against the effects of the economic crisis. These initiatives were instrumental, directly and indirectly, in creating the movements that brought to the March on Washington the 75,000 trade unionists on April 26th. But in spite of all this, many states and cities do not have meaningful coalitions around these economic issues, we have very few examples of neighborhood coalitions or state-wide coalitions. This is true even in the areas where the devastation has been the most severe. Thus, on the economic front these are areas where there is a vacuum, a need for leadership.

Important coalitions have been developed in certain election campaigns, and especially in those of a more local area—including the campaigns of Mark Allen, Alva Buxenbaum and Amadeo Richardson, as well as in New Haven, Boston and in a number of cities. Yet, even in this field we do not have coalitions on a state scale, although in past years, we had such coalitions on specific issues for a temporary period, such as on taxes in Ohio.

We can learn from all these experiences, and take many bold initiatives to meet today's crisis problems. We can also draw some lessons from the willingness of people to join in broad sponsoring committees, especially on the issues of inflation and unemployment—and the November 16th action in 40 cities was an important coalition development.

Any Party organization—be it on a club, city, state or national level—that is not involved, does not take the initiative and provide leadership in building forms, coalitions, alliances, forms of organization, or does not take initiatives to concretely take up the economic problems facing the people, is not fulfilling its vanguard role, and will remain isolated and live in a sectarian shell.

It is in this same sense, and in the context of filling vacuums, that we must see the indispensable role of the Young Workers Liberation League (YWLL). In many ways it is filling the vacuum in the youth field. As odd as it may seem, I'm afraid that many in our Party are not aware of the growth and influence of the YWLL.

I don't remember when I was more inspired, felt a greater sense of pride or a deeper sense of confidence as I experienced at the last national YWLL Convention which was attended by 750 young delegates and invited guests.

The prospect of "jobless generations" and the accompanying accelerating development of mass radicalization of the youth make both necessary and possible the rapid growth of a mass YWLL. Such a development of the YWLL meets the needs of the youth, the working class and the Party.

The YWLL has proven its ability to unite broad sections of youth—young workers, racially oppressed youth and high school and college youth, in struggle for their needs in connection with the building of Youth United for Jobs (YUJ) groups in 14 cities.

The youth contingents of the Nattional Coalition to Fight Inflation and Unemployment at the April 26th March on Washington and the contingent in the April 4th march against racism were very impressive. The YWLL works to build a youth front of this generation to fight for the "right to earn, learn and live." It provides the youth movement with a working-class hinge. It is now moving sizable numbers of youth, and can move many more who are searching for radical answers—who are looking toward Marxism-Leninism and socialism and, therefore toward the Communist Party.

We need to step up our efforts to assist the YWLL realize its potential in the current situation. This means helping to move the labor movement and all other people's forces to support the special demands of youth for summer jobs and jobs in general. Adult working people are deeply concerned that their children will be provided a real opportunity to "earn, learn and live."

This means we must assist the League in developing its own youthful and flexible style of work and a stronger orientation toward the more youthful sections of the young generation. This means we must assist the League in their educational work and in the crucial development of cadre for League work.

We must face the hard fact that we cannot fulfill the leadership vacuum in the youth arena without a strong YWLL.

There are many other areas in which we are not satisfactorily filling the leadership vacuum.

There are some very important stirrings in the field of culture.

There is a rising mood of struggle and an important sector of the cultural movement is developing a militancy and a close kinship with the mass movements in the country—including the struggle against imperialism and racism. This cultural upsurge is also developing a close relationship with the working class movement.

We have taken some steps in the field of culture, including the national Party conference and the continuing publication of a very fine, popular newsletter that has turned into an excellent cultural magazine. And there is some very good work being done by some art and cultural projects, including the movement here in Chicago around the painting of outdoor mass murals, in addition to other activities. But we are not measuring up to the tasks or the upsurge. Leadership attention to the cultural field is an absolute necessity. It is an indispensable ingredient of the mass strugggles, of the anti-monopoly, anti-racist democratic movements. The cultural movement is a most important contingent in the struggle for socialism. We must take steps to fill this vacuum of leadership in this field.

The same is true in the area of farm work. The Draft Political Resolution, with many of its weaknesses, is in our opinion, a beginning in filling the leadership vacuum in this field. But to continue this work we must set up a structure, both within the Party and for mass work, in the farm communities. We must not only reject ideas that there are no farmers who can be won over to struggle, but begin serious work with farms. There are many examples of struggles of the farmers. The monopolies are as much an enemy of the small and middle farmers as they are of the industrial workers.

There is a vacuum in our work in such fields as public education. This is largely left to some comrades who are teachers or who work in this field. It is an important area in which the Party as a whole must find ways of giving leadership.

Mass Education

We have generally improved our work in mass education. But in spite of this the vacuum, or the gap, is growing. We are not keeping up with the potential that this moment presents.

The present crisis affords an excellent opportunity for raising the level of class consciousness of the workers. Though political struggle is the major road to class consciousness, it is not separate from simultaneous propaganda and agitation. We cannot say that education is our strong point from the standpoint of the masses.

Ideas are a mobilizing force. And Communist ideas, both fundamental and immediate, are indispensable for elevating the struggle in the country.

During this last year we have greatly increased the circulation of the *Daily World* and *People's World*. But they are not yet instruments of mass education, agitation and propaganda. To fill the vacuum, their circulation should reach into the hundreds of thousands. That is a new concept, in keeping with the mass upsurge in the thinking of millions who want to know why the millions of Italians in the recent elections voted for the Communist Party, and together with the Socialist Party, they are at the top.

To fill the vacuum in mass education we need popular mass pamphlets on such burning questions as the economic crisis.

To close the gap we must put an end to sectarian concepts of the role of the science of Marxism-Leninism. Too often mass pamphlets are viewed as inner-Party property, something we use internally to analyze objective events. We underestimate the desire of the masses for such literature. Such a concept is not in step with the level of today's mass movements. Often when we write about Marxism-Leninism, the language and style of the material is obviously meant only for ourselves. It is written in a very special inner-Party language. Let us open this great body of thought to workers, to masses generally. When we do not present this great science to the people, the phonies step into the vacuum with their dogmatic, distorted, sectarian concepts.

We need to have popular pamphlets on basic features of Marxism-Leninism. We should open up and initiate public mass dialogues. More schools and seminars, open to all who want to study this great science can help meet the desire of workers for this basic knowledge.

The press must have popular features on Marxism-Leninism. Marxism-Leninism is a mass ideology and should be regularly featured in the mass media. A fight to establish departments of Marxism-Leninism in colleges is in order, following the example of the University of Minnesota. As an additional example, this is the third year that the New School for Social Research in New York City has been giving a 3-credit undergraduate course in the "Fundamentals of Marxism" by an active Marxist, who was Chairman of the Economics and Politics Department of the Jefferson School of Social Science. And the New School bulletin notes this fact, as well as his political activism in Cuba work and civil liberties.

Political Affairs should become a much more popular organ, packaging the ideas of the science of Marxism-Leninism in a manner that will excite and educate broad sectors of the people.

Routinism is a drag in all fields of work. But in the field of mass education, mass agitation and propaganda it is a most deadly weakness. To be in a rut is to be nowhere.

We have greatly improved our work in the area of ideology. Our Party is not only politically united. We have oneness ideologically. To reach this level, along the way we had to reject the revisionist idea that it is not necessary for the Party to fight for oneness in ideology. But we need to continue being on top of these ideological challenges. We need a continuing struggle for ideas, approaches, for styles of work which are associated with the working class. We need to develop working class characteristics in our leadership cadre. This means a struggle against all of the petty-bourgeois baggage of individualism, elitism, immodesty, the lack of ability to work collectively, low moral and ethical standards of behavior—which all adds to bureaucratic attitudes and methods of work.

A revolutionary working-class party must have a leading cadre that represents and reflects the best of our class.

We have made important headway against the seepage of racism and white chauvinism into our Party's ranks. But we cannot afford to be complacent for many reasons.

There are the dialectical two sides: new opportunities in the struggle against racism, as well as the continuing efforts by the ruling class to inject this poison into the lifestream of our society. As the crisis contradictions sharpen, the racist pressures increase. And the same sharpening of the contradictions gives rise to struggles that become a pressure for greater unity, which in turn helps to create the objective conditions in which the fight against the racist pressures can be more successful.

To meet this situation it is necessary for the Party to raise to new levels its role among the white sections of the working class and other white masses, to win them to struggle against the oppression and discrimination against Black and other nationally oppressed peoples, and against the influence of ruling class racism. This is a condition, a necessary feature in a successful struggle against reaction in general, which includes their own best self-interests. And connected with our ability to do this, and for the Party to be able to exert leadership by example among the masses, it must raise sharply the level of understanding internally, and the struggle against all manifestations of white chauvinism in its own ranks.

The primary test of whether we are making real progress should be the initiative of white Communists among white masses on today's decisive front with respect to racism, jobs and the economic crisis. This means setting concrete goals, with checkup and control, in placing demands and winning over white masses to support them for: special jobs creation programs for the victims of racism; the fight to modify seniority to break the last-to-be-hired, first-to-be-fired pattern, etc. It means rejecting the liberal and Social Democratic pressures to place the demand for full employment in such a way that it becomes an excuse for not fighting for the special demands of Black workers.

Since the ruling class is making the fight against busing their main front to divide and divert white working masses, this calls for new initiatives by our white comrades among white masses as a concrete test of our progress, setting tasks with specific checkup and control.

Our internal educational work, running from the basics on racism and the national question to the typical forms of the expression of white chauvinism in our ranks, must be raised to a new level.

To tolerate manifestations of white chauvinism, to have a liberal attitude toward acts of chauvinism, is to increase the seepage of the poison. The task is not only to put an end to the manifestations, but to burn out the ideological influence of white chauvinism that brought on the manifestations in the first place.

Zionism, as a bourgeois ideological current, continues to surface as a more serious problem. It is a very active, reactionary force working on all levels of our society. In the past years it has been increasingly able to misuse sentiments that stem from the experience of anti-Semitism, and the support and pride that Jewish masses feel for Israel as a country. Zionism has become a greater problem because of its policy of utilizing these mass currents.

Because of the events in the Mideast and the Soviet Union's strong anti-imperialist stand, the Zionist propaganda is extremely and viciously anti-Soviet.

This problem has been further complicated in the left ranks of the Jewish community by the capitulation and opportunistic accommodation to all these Zionist and reactionary nationalist currents by the editors of the *Morning Freiheit.*

Our comrades in the field of Jewish work are doing some very good work. They are beginning to fill the vacuum in this area, including the publication of *Jewish Affairs.* We must continue the struggle against these reactionary and opportunistic currents.

But while doing so we must guard against some weaknesses, weaknesses that appear from a one-sidedness. We are against the ideology and the policies of Zionism including their definition of anti-Semitism. But we are the most consistent fighters against anti-Semitism. We are against the policies of aggression pursued by the Zionist leaders of Israel. But we have, in the most consistent and principled manner, supported Israel's right to live in peace within the established 1967 borders. When we take issue with the reactionary currents (and we need to strengthen our ideological struggle against Zionism and expose the Zionist danger to peace and to the people of Israel), we must make absolutely sure no one can inadvertently or deliberately misinterpret our positions as giving support to anti-Semitism. This is in line with our Party's principled stand against racism, great power chauvinism and anti-Semitism.

One of the new questions with an ideological backdrop is the question of "planning under capitalism." Sections of monopoly capital, some leaders of trade unions, and young liberals have picked on this as the new panacea. It has especially attracted labor leaders who are looking for a way to differentiate themselves from Meany.

They call for long-term "planning" of monopoly capitalism—they say the cause of all the trouble is "lack of information." They ignore the question of who is going to benefit from such planning. Monopoly capital is not against planning if they are the beneficiaries. They do not want to change any of the present relationships. They do not call for nationalization or for workers' control, or for higher wages, tax cuts, or to control inflation, or to eliminate the racist patterns in industry.

The motivating thought of this "planning" is class collaboration. It is an attempt to overcome some of the rough spots of state-monopoly capitalism.

These 5-year plans are not in any way related to socialist planning.

We are for planning where it helps the working class gain employment, reduce prices, democratize the work place, have a say in what is produced, how fast, and under what conditions. We are *not* for planning which protects and encourages corporate profits. We want planning which involves nationalization, under the most democratic control possible, not for planning which helps private companies win greater and more consistent profits.

We must say quite frankly that lack of "information" is *not* the main problem causing poor performance of the capitalist economy. Therefore, planning mechanisms which rely on "information" as the persuader will fail.

One of the questions that invariably comes up in every press conference or public appearance is: what are your Party's relations with the world Communist movement? In most cases this is still the shadow of the old slander of whether we are a foreign dominated party. We have not yet fully dispersed the fog of anti-communism. Usually my answer is that our relations with the other Parties are very good. They are comradely and friendly. We are for ever closer, fraternal, comradely relations.

As a matter of fact we are very much in favor of another world meeting of Communist Parties as soon as possible. We believe the new stage of developments in the world should get the collective attention of the world Communist movement. In the relationship with the world Communist movement we contribute to and we learn from such exchanges and experiences.

We are not just another political party. We represent the working class, the leading and the only revolutionary class in this period of history. As a revolutionary party we have unique tasks. Our theories, our politics, our tactics, the structure of our Party and our discipline are all geared to fulfilling that historic task.

We are also unique in the way we view ourselves. We do not cover up. We do not overlook our own weaknesses. Criticism and self-criticism are integral features of being a Communist. They are methods of political and ideological growth and development. They are ways of nipping a shortcoming in the bud, before it starts to fester, before it becomes a major problem.

We are unique in that we speak of our weaknesses publicly. People should be told the truth, Lenin said, and generally they will draw the right conclusions: "If . . . we are not afraid to speak the sad and bitter truth straight out we shall learn, we shall unfailingly and certainly learn to overcome all our difficulties." (Lenin, *Collected Works*, Vol. 33, p. 98.)

We must continue to develop this Leninist art of criticism and self-criticism. In a sense it is also a vacuum that must be filled.

But as with all phenomena, the single is related to and a part of the whole. Therefore, in a voluntary organization like our Party, with every right there is a corresponding responsibility. So Lenin added: "Every one is free to write and say whatever he likes without any restrictions. But every voluntary association (including a party) is also free to expel members who use the name of the party to advocate anti-party views." (Lenin, *Collected Works*, Vol. 10, p. 47.)

From some of the new revelations about the FBI we have learned something which we have really always known—that the enemy agent also uses the right of criticism in the Party. They use the right to slander and disrupt and to keep the Party involved in a constant condition of internal wrangling. This of course puts an additional responsibility on Communists. How to be critical, but not disruptive; how to examine things critically, but not create a platform for the enemy agent; how to open up weaknesses for discussion, but not open the doors to the enemy agent. This is a responsibility all Communists must accept.

The right of criticism must be placed within the democratic structure that once a majority has come to conclusions the minority must abide by such decisions. All this has to be considered within the context that we are all responsible for the unity and for the fighting *esprit de corps* of our Party. Unity and a spirited atmosphere are necessary conditions for building the Party.

Party Building

As was said before, we have come a hell of a long way. But we must complete that thought. We must add a qualifying phrase—that we have come a hell of a long way but not far enough and not nearly as far as we could have.

The Draft Main Political Resolution has a section on why we have not gone far enough in building the Party. What is bothersome is that in the very excellent and extensive pre-Convention discussions we have had on the Draft Resolution the part of the Resolution on the building of the Party did not receive much attention.

The 200-some new members who we have recruited as a feature of the Convention preparations are proof of the fact that we are right about the possibilities of Party building. The increase in the circulation of the press is evidence of the growing range of the Party's influence. But I think it is an absolute necessity that we now give Party building a new status on the list of our political and organizational priorities. We must now raise it from the status of being very important to the status of being *the most important.*

This must become the priority at all levels of the Party. We must take the question of Party building out of the secondary, the follow-up slot, and place it where it belongs—as a simultaneous and continuing prerequisite to successfully fulfilling our mass tasks, as a contribution to strengthening the mass people's struggles.

Without a bigger Party there is a built-in weakness, a built-in limitation within all mass movements. It is a hard fact of political reality—the potential of any mass movement cannot reach full fruition without the unique input of the Communist Party. Without this input, movements will flounder in the fog of reformist illusions, they will flay away, without aim or targets.

I spoke about the art of self-criticism. In that spirit I think we have to say that which very often goes unmentioned. And that is that there is something fundamentally politically and ideologically wrong with a Communist who is active, who relates to mass work, but who does not recruit members to our Party. It is a good place to start developing the art of criticism and self-criticism.

If we agree that our analysis of the moment and the accompanying mass upsurge is correct, then it seems to me we have to put our own house in order. We have to think in terms of political breakthroughs. We have to organize the work of the Party in terms of a qualitative turning point. The concepts of what mass work is in this period, the concept of what is possible and necessary in order to get our literature and press to the people, of what is possible in terms of Party building, must be brought into step with the historic potential of this moment— this turning point in history. This is the central challenge facing our Party and this 21st National Convention.

The events, the trends, the currents of history are not saying— take it easy, everything is coming up roses anyway. Their message is clear. You are now swimming with the tides of history. It is much easier, but you still have to swim and, at times, against strong counter-currents.

ILLUSTRATIONS

Henry Winston, National Chairman; Gus Hall, General Secretary; and Kendra Alexander, Organizational Secretary of the CP of Northern California.

SCENES FROM THE CONVENTION

Joelle Fishman, Executive Secretary of the CP of Connecticut.

Grace Mora, Chairperson of the Puerto Rican Liberation Commission.

Top—Angela Davis. Bottom—L to R—Gus Hall, Angela Davis, Henry Winston, Mike Zagarell, Jack Kling, James Steele.

Rally Chairpersons—Alva Buxenbaum, Chairperson of the National Commission on Women's Equality, and Jack Kling, Executive Secretary of the CP of Illinois-Iowa.

James Steele, National Chairman, Young Workers Liberation League.

Among the audience.

Political Rock.

RALLY SCENES

A Grip on the Future.

The Young Generation in Action.

Honoring Charter-founding Members of the CPUSA.

Felix Ojeda, General Secretary,
Communist Party of Puerto Rico.

William Ross, Central Committee member,
Communist Party of Canada.

AN EVENING OF INTERNATIONAL SOLIDARITY

Mass Rally.

Against the Fascist Junta in Chile.

FIGHTING ON
THE ISSUES

For Women's Equality.

Vietnam Peace March.

For Jobs and Economic Justice.

For the Independence of Puerto Rico.

For Detente.

WALDHEIM CEMETERY, CHICAGO— BURIAL PLACE OF THE HAYMARKET MARTYRS AND COMMUNIST LEADERS

At the monument to leaders of the CPUSA—L to R—Dan Spector, Henry Winston, Fern Winston, Ken Newcomb.

At the grave site of a founder of the CPUSA—L to R— Michele Stone, Helen Winter, Henry Winston, Fern Winston.